The Records of the Universalist Church of Spencer, Massachusetts, 1876-1911

Sandra Goodwin

Goodwin
Genealogy
Productions

Cover design: author
Publishing company logo: 777images

Printed in the United States of America

First Printing, 2020

ISBN 978-1-7351931-1-3
Library of Congress Control Number: 2020914858

Goodwin Genealogy Productions
P. O. Box 124
Leicester, Massachusetts 01524

This book is dedicated to
CARLA SULLIVAN,
a dedicated MSOG member,
who left us to pursue her ancestors
on a higher plane.

TABLE OF CONTENTS

ACKNOWLEDGMENTS

I would like to thank the following members, current and former, of the Massachusetts Society of Genealogists for their help with the transcription of these records:

Ina Armstrong
Carol Bacon
Herb Cole
Joan Croteau
Gordo Elliot
Paul Holzwarth
Hazel Miele

Mary Elizabeth Noone
Linda Pelletier
Rebecca Rector
Carla Sullivan
Tom Swan
Gail Terry
Jacques Travers

Many thanks also to Jean Mulhall, former town clerk of Spencer, Massachusetts, for her support of this project.

INTRODUCTION

While helping to catalog the contents of "the vault" in the Spencer (Massachusetts) Town Hall, my cousin Lori Anthony and I came across a small box up on a top shelf wrapped in brown paper and secured with twine. The label on the box was addressed to the Spencer Town Clerk. The Universalist Church of Spencer, no longer in existence, sent it to the Town Hall in the 1940s.

Inside were the records of the Universalist Church from its beginnings in the 1870s to the closing of its doors in the 1940s.

When we unwrapped and opened the box, we found several church books with information dating from 1876-1911. A book that I refer to as Book 1 contained the records of the church. There were lists of pastors, deacons, members of the Ladies' Circle, and Sunday school superintendents. For the most part, these lists seemed to be incomplete. They were followed by the membership lists and records of baptisms, marriages, and burials. Another book which I refer to as Book 2 duplicated many of the records from Book 1. However, sometimes there was information found in Book 1 but not in Book 2; sometimes there was information in Book 2 that was not in Book 1. This has been noted where applicable.

The records from Book 1 and Book 2 were transcribed by members of the Massachusetts Society of Genealogists. Those transcriptions make up the bulk of this book. However, the box contained other books, loose papers, and letters, the contents of which are described beginning on the next page should anyone wish to pursue their research in more depth.

You will also see references to several villages in the area. Within the town of Spencer are the villages of South Spencer, Hillsville, and Wire Village. Podunk refers to an unincorporated area mostly within the neighboring town of East Brookfield.

Universalist Church Records—Other Books

1) Church of Our Father Universalist: Return to E. F. Sibley, Spencer, Mass.

> May 31, 1882: Church support pledges—includes person's name and his/her weekly pledge (3 pages)
>
> November 1, 1903: Church support pledges—includes person's name and his/her weekly pledge (5 pages)
>
> July 1903: Pledges from church members toward the expenses of Rev. F. L. Masseck at summer school at Clark University (2 pages)
>
> November 19, 1903: Pledge to purchase Harmonies (new & old) (4 pages)
>
> November 26, 1903: Pledges to pay toward church debt (1 page)
>
> June 29, 1904: Pledges to pay toward church debt (8 pages)
>
> Church Water Meter after pipe was repaired (2 pages)
>
> Lists of members by street (22 pages)

2) Pierce's Memorandum and Account Book (inside front cover of red book)

> Donations toward church building and payments toward building from 1881 to 1884

3) Red Book

> Alphabetical listing of members along with tax and premium paid for the years 1885-1891; includes pew rental receipts

4) Secretary's Book: Universalist Missionery Society, Spencer, Mass.

> Includes the constitution, officers, members, minutes, and treasurer's report of the Women's Mission Circle of the Church of Our Father from 1905-1916. Includes some death and burial information about members.

5) Pew Rental Book

> Tax, premium, and amount paid for pew rental by month from 1890-94

6) Treasurer's Records: Church of Our Father Universalist, Spencer, Mass.

> From 1898-1936; includes financial information regarding the dissolution of the church

7) Black Book (includes Constitution of the Church)

Includes Constitution, members list, by-laws, application for corporation, minutes of meetings, and building contract for the church, 1881-1910

October 30, 1878: Church support pledges—includes person's name and his/her weekly pledge (3 pages)

May 1, 1876: Church support pledges—includes person's name and his/her weekly pledge (2 pages)

8) Black Book, red trim—Minutes

Minutes of meetings from 1910-1945

Includes letter dated 1936 regarding the sale of the church property and dissolution of the church

9) Various loose papers

Pledges from church members to carpet the church

A letter from Henry L. Watson documenting the history of the church, dated 1893

Deed to a pew dated 1831, Isaac Lamb administrator for the estate of Jonathan White, sold to Sylvester Luther [there had been an earlier church]

Booklet with member donations/pledges

May 26, 1880: Church support pledges—includes person's name and his/her weekly pledge (2 pages)

May 25, 1881: Church support pledges— includes person's name and his/her weekly pledge (2 pages)

Pledges from church members to buy a lot on Linden St. and build the church, dated 1881

Pledges from church members to purchase an organ

Two letters from W. A. Stickney

~~~~~~~~~~~~~~~~~~~~~~~~~~~~~~~~~~~~~~

BOOK 1

~~~~~~~~~~~~~~~~~~~~~~~~~~~~~~~~~~~~~~

~~~~~~~~~~~~~~~~~~~~~~
PASTOR NOTES
~~~~~~~~~~~~~~~~~~~~~~

Information on the pastors of the Universalist Church of Spencer are located in what will be referred to as Book 1 (see introduction), pages 6 and 7. This section was divided into nine columns with the following headings: line number, name, birthplace, date of birth, college, place of theological education, date of ordination, date of installation, and date and mode of removal. The "date of ordination" heading was crossed out, with no substitution put in its place.

All dates have been changed to standard form for punctuation. Ex: Jan 5- 1899 became January 5, 1899.

All other abbreviations and spellings are retained as per the original.

~~~~~~~~~~~~~~~~~~~~~~
PASTORS
~~~~~~~~~~~~~~~~~~~~~~

Line #: 0
Name: Walter S. Vail—Mr. Vail was never installed as pastor. He was the first regular worker in this place, coming from Tufts Divinity School where he was a student.
Place of Theological Education: Tufts
Date of Ordination: Began work here February 27, 1876
Date and mode of removal: Resigned. Preached farewell sermon April 15, 1877. Died 1907.

~~~~~~~~~~~~~~~~~~~~

Line #: 1
Name: Fredrick A Bisbee, D. D.
BirthPlace: Nunda, N. Y.
Date of birth: 1855
Place of Theological Education: Tufts
Date of Ordination: June 19, 1877
Date of Installation: June 19, 1877
Date and mode of removal: Resigned 1883

~~~~~~~~~~~~~~~~~~~~

4

Line #: 2
Name: Chas. A. Knickerbocker
College: Tufts
Place of Theological Education: Tufts
Date of Ordination: Began work July 1, 1883
Date of Installation: 1885
Date and mode of removal: Died August 8, 1929

~~~~~~~~~~~~~~~~~~

Line #: 3
Name: John M. Bartholomew
College: Tufts (1881)
Place of Theological Education: Tufts (1884)
Date of Ordination: called July 28, 1885
Date of Installation: 1888
Date and mode of removal: Died December 9, 1906

~~~~~~~~~~~~~~~~~~

Line #: 4
Name: Jos. S. Gledhill
BirthPlace: Lucas, Ohio
Date of birth: July 30, 1848
Place of Theological Education: Canton (1876)
Date of Ordination: 1876; called November 1, 1888
Date and mode of removal: Resigned February 23, to take effect May 1, 1892; Retired from Ministry

~~~~~~~~~~~~~~~~~~

Line #: 5
Name: Thomas O. Marvin
College: Tufts
Place of Theological Education: Tufts
Date of Ordination: April 1889; called August 1, 1892
Date of Installation: 1892
Date and mode of removal: Resigned October 1, to take effect December 1, 1894; Retired from Ministry 1900

~~~~~~~~~~~~~~~~~~

Line #: 6
Name: C. W. Biddle, D. D.
BirthPlace: Chesapeake City, Md.
Date of birth: December 3, 1832
Date of Ordination: called March 15, 1895
Date and mode of removal: Resigned May 27, 1896; Died August 4, 1900

~~~~~~~~~~~~~~~~~~

Line #: 7
Name: Flint M. Bissell
BirthPlace: Wilmington, Vt.
Date of birth: September 8, 1866
Place of Theological Education: Tufts (1897)
Date of Ordination: June 1897; called March 16, 1897
Date of Installation: September 1897; (called in March, and began work at once)
Date and mode of removal: Resigned July 31, 1898

~~~~~~~~~~~~~~~~~~

Line #: 8
Name: Edward C. Downey
BirthPlace: Ft. Jackson, N. Y.
Date of birth: April 29, 1870
Place of Theological Education:
Canton (1895)
Date of Ordination: March 19,
1896; called September 12, 1898
Date of Installation: October 14,
1898
Date and mode of removal:
Resigned November 1900

~~~~~~~~~~~~~~~~~~

Line #: 9
Name: George W. Fuller
BirthPlace: Charlestown, Mass.
Date of birth: November 17,
1876
Place of Theological Education:
Tufts (1901)
Date of Ordination: called
February 28, 1901
Date and mode of removal:
Resigned, March 9, 1902

~~~~~~~~~~~~~~~~~~

Line #: 10
Name: Frank Lincoln Masseck
BirthPlace: Milford, N. H.
Date of birth: March 12, 1865
Place of Theological Education:
Canton, N. Y. (1888)
Date of Ordination: September
27, 1888
Date of Installation: May 6,
1902 (Began work April 1)
Date and mode of removal:
Resigned, April 30, 1905

Line #: 11
Name: Asa M. Bradley
BirthPlace: Brewster, Mass.
Date of birth: March 9, 1856
Date of Ordination: June 2, 1895
Date of Installation: December
1, 1905; Began work as [supply?]
Date and mode of removal:
Service ended February 1, 1910;
Died January 20, 1936

~~~~~~~~~~~~~~~~~~

Line #: 12
Name: Dr. George L. Perin
Date of Ordination: September
25, 1910

~~~~~~~~~~~~~~~~~~

Line #: 13
Name: George F. Babbitt

~~~~~~~~~~~~~~~~~~

Line #: 14
Name: George F. Morton
Date of Ordination: December
26, 1915
Date and mode of removal:
Services ended January 1, 1918

DEACON NOTES

Information on the deacons of the Universalist Church are located in Book 1, page 10. This section was divided into five columns with the following headings: line number, name, appointed, ceased to act, and remarks. The records are obviously incomplete.

DEACONS

#: 1
Name: A. N. Lamb
Appointed: January 4, 1878
Ceased to Act: Resigned March 22, 1883

#: 2
Name: E. F. Sibley
Appointed: March 22, 1883

#: 3
Name: Van R. Kent
Appointed: March 22, 1883
Ceased to Act: March 23, 1891
Remarks: See page 30

#: 4
Name: A. N. Lamb
Appointed: April 4, 1890

LADIES CIRCLE NOTES

Information on members of the Ladies Circle is located on page 22 of Book 1. This section was divided into five columns with the following headings: line number, year, president, secretary, and Y.R.C.U. (There is only one entry in this last column, on line 20.)

Nothing was written under "President" from the year 1903 to 1905, and nothing was under "Secretary" from 1901 to 1905. Whether ditto marks were forgotten or these positions were not filled for those years is unknown at this time.

LADIES CIRCLE

Line #: 3
Year: 1883
Pres.: Mrs. Ira E. Lackey
Sec.: Mrs. E. F. Sibley

Line #: 4
Year: 1884
Pres.: Mrs. Ira E. Lackey
Sec.: Mrs. I. Slayton

Line #: 5
Year: 1885
Pres.: Mrs. Ira E. Lackey
Sec.: Mrs. I. Slayton

~~~~~~~~~~~~~~~~~~

Line #: 6
Year: 1886
Pres.: Mrs. Ira E. Lackey
Sec.: Mrs. I. Slayton

~~~~~~~~~~~~~~~~~~

Line #: 7
Year: 1887
Pres.: Mrs. Ira E. Lackey
Sec.: Mrs. I. Slayton

~~~~~~~~~~~~~~~~~~

Line #: 8
Year: 1888
Pres.: Mrs. E. H. Howland
Sec.: Mrs. C. H. Newton

~~~~~~~~~~~~~~~~~~

Line #: 9
Year: 1889
Pres.: Mrs. E. H. Howland
Sec.: Mrs. C. H. Newton

~~~~~~~~~~~~~~~~~~

Line #: 10
Year: 1890
Pres.: Mrs. E. H. Howland
Sec.: Mrs. C. H. Newton

~~~~~~~~~~~~~~~~~~

Line #: 11
Year: 1891
Pres.: Mrs. E. H. Howland
Sec.: Mrs. C. H. Newton

~~~~~~~~~~~~~~~~~~

Line #: 12
Year: 1892
Pres.: Mrs. E. H. Howland
Sec.: Mrs. E. H. Slayton

~~~~~~~~~~~~~~~~~~

Line #: 13
Year: 1893
Pres.: Mrs. E. H. Howland
Sec.: Mrs. G. W. Morse

~~~~~~~~~~~~~~~~~~

Line #: 14
Year: 1894
Pres.: Mrs. E. H. Howland
Sec.: Mrs. E. Warren

~~~~~~~~~~~~~~~~~~

Line #: 15
Year: 1895
Pres.: Mrs. C. W. Myrick
Sec.: Mrs. E. Warren

~~~~~~~~~~~~~~~~~~

Line #: 16
Year: 1896
Pres.: Mrs. C. W. Myrick
Sec.: Miss E. J. Allen

~~~~~~~~~~~~~~~~~~

Line #: 17
Year: 1897
Pres.: Mrs. E. Warren
Sec.: Mrs. E. R. Wheeler

~~~~~~~~~~~~~~~~~~

Line #: 18
Year: 1898
Pres.: Mrs. E. Warren
Sec.: Miss Hanscom; Mrs. Paul Sibley

~~~~~~~~~~~~~~~~~~

Line #: 19
Year: 1899
Pres.: Mrs. E. Warren
Sec.: Miss Hanscom; Mrs. Paul Sibley

~~~~~~~~~~~~~~~~~~

Line #: 20
Year: 1900
Pres.: Mrs. Sarah Prouty
Sec.: Mrs. W. H. Potter
Y.R.C.U.: Miss Eva Fales; Miss Carrie Sibley

~~~~~~~~~~~~~~~~~~

Line #: 21
Year: 1901
Pres.: Mrs. Sarah Prouty

~~~~~~~~~~~~~~~~~~

Line #: 22
Year: 1902
Pres.: Mrs. Sarah Prouty

Line #: 23
Year: 1903

~~~~~~~~~~~~~~~~~~

Line #: 24
Year: 1904

~~~~~~~~~~~~~~~~~~

Line #: 25
Year: 1905

~~~~~~~~~~~~~~~~~~

Line #: 26
Year: 1906
Pres.: Mrs. Sarah Prouty
Sec.: Mrs. Eleanor Davis

~~~~~~~~~~~~~~~~~~

Line #: 27
Year: 1907
Pres.: Mrs. W. H. Potter
Sec.: Mrs. Carrie Bemis

~~~~~~~~~~~~~~~~~~

SUNDAY SCHOOL SUPERINTENDENT NOTES

~~~~~~~~~~~~~~~~~~

Information on the Sunday school superintendents of the Universalist Church are located in Book 1, page 18. This section is divided into three columns with the following headings: line number, name, when chosen. The information is obviously incomplete.

~~~~~~~~~~~~~~~~~~~~~~

SUNDAY SCHOOL
SUPERINTENDENTS

~~~~~~~~~~~~~~~~~~~~~~

Line #: 1
Name: A. N. Lamb
When chosen: June 1, 1876

~~~~~~~~~~~~~~~~~~

Line #: 2
Name: E. F. Sibley

~~~~~~~~~~~~~~~~~~~

Line #: 3
Name: Van R. Kent

~~~~~~~~~~~~~~~~~~~

Line #: 4
Name: E. F. Sibley

~~~~~~~~~~~~~~~~~~~

Line #: 5
Name: L. H. Bacon

~~~~~~~~~~~~~~~~~~~~~

MEMBERS NOTES

~~~~~~~~~~~~~~~~~~~~~

Information on the members of the Universalist Church are located in Book 1, page 30-41. There are ten columns with the following headings: line number, name, day and month received into the church, year received, how received, day and month removed, year removed, how removed, remarks, and additional information found only in Book 2 (see introduction).

It is noted in the membership section that members 1-20 are the twenty original members.

Book 2 lists persons #39-59 as being received into the Church by the pastor Rev. J. M. Bartholomew; persons #60-78 received by Rev. J. S. Gledhill, pastor; persons #79-83 received by T. O. Marvin; and persons #84-103 by C. W. Biddle.

For females, their names were originally entered as they appeared at the time they were received into the church. If that woman later married, very often someone went back into the record and added the married name. Sometimes her husband's given name is recorded.

Standardized punctuation was used. [ ] indicates words added by the editor. [ ] around data indicates a best guess as to what was written. The "Additions from Book 2" column includes spelling variations.

The '"Remarks" column seemed to be a place for recording street addresses (ex: Main; 25 Mech-anic) or forwarding addresses (ex: Brookline; Washington, DC).

Dates were transcribed as they appeared in the original.

~~~~~~~~~~~~~~~~~~~~~~

MEMBERS

~~~~~~~~~~~~~~~~~~~~~~

Line #: 1
Name: Cynthia A. Bacon
Reception Date: Jan. 4, 1878
Removal Date: Sept. 29, 1901
How removed: Died

~~~~~~~~~~~~~~~~~~

Line #: 2
Name: Myra W. Sibley
Reception Date: Jan. 4, 1878
Removal Date: July, 1887
How removed: Died
Additional information from Book 2: Mary W. Sibley

~~~~~~~~~~~~~~~~~~

Line #: 3
Name: David A. Drury
Reception Date: Jan. 4, 1878
How removed: Died

~~~~~~~~~~~~~~~~~~

Line #: 4
Name: Electa N. Drury
Reception Date: Jan. 4, 1878
Remarks: 78 Main

~~~~~~~~~~~~~~~~~~

Line #: 5
Name: E. Harris Howland
Reception Date: Jan. 4, 1878

Remarks: 31 Pleasant

~~~~~~~~~~~~~~~~~~

Line #: 6
Name: Mrs Nancy Hale
Reception Date: Jan. 4, 1878
How removed: Died

~~~~~~~~~~~~~~~~~~

Line #: 7
Name: Emory F. Sibley
Reception Date: Jan. 4, 1878
Remarks: 640 Washington St., Brookline

~~~~~~~~~~~~~~~~~~

Line #: 8
Name: Mary P. Sibley
Reception Date: Jan. 4, 1878

~~~~~~~~~~~~~~~~~~

Line #: 9
Name: Oscar W. Wilson
Reception Date: Jan. 4, 1878
Removal Date: June 11, 1904
How removed: Died

~~~~~~~~~~~~~~~~~~

Line #: 10
Name: Lidia A. Wilson
Reception Date: Jan. 4, 1878
Remarks: So. Spencer

~~~~~~~~~~~~~~~~~~

Line #: 11
Name: Martha A. Wilson
Reception Date: Jan. 4, 1878
Removal Date: April 22, 1907
How removed: Died
Remarks: Died in Sanatorium in Burlington, Vt.
Additional information from Book 2: sister t. o. w.

~~~~~~~~~~~~~~~~~~

Line #: 12
Name: William Doane
Reception Date: Jan. 4, 1878
Removal Date: Aug 1, 1904
How removed: Died
Remarks: Died in Sanatorium in Burlington, Vt.
Additional information from Book 2: old; So. Spencer, near o. w. w.

~~~~~~~~~~~~~~~~~~

Line #: 13
Name: Gertrude E. Doane
Reception Date: Jan. 4, 1878
Removal Date: July, 1883
How removed: Died

~~~~~~~~~~~~~~~~~~

Line #: 14
Name: Elizabeth Bemis
Reception Date: Jan. 4, 1878
Removal Date: May 18, 1905
How removed: Died
Remarks: 43 Pleasant
Additional information from Book 2: Mrs. Joshua

Line #: 15
Name: Emiline Bemis
Reception Date: Jan. 4, 1878
Removal Date: 1902
How removed: Died
Additional information from Book 2: Emeline

~~~~~~~~~~~~~~~~~~

Line #: 16
Name: Harriet E. Adams
Reception Date: Jan. 4, 1878
Remarks: 40 Pleasant

~~~~~~~~~~~~~~~~~~

Line #: 17
Name: Rebecca A. Livermore
Reception Date: Jan. 4, 1878
How removed: Died
Remarks: 19 Grove
Additional information from Book 2: Mrs. Warren L.

~~~~~~~~~~~~~~~~~~

Line #: 18
Name: Ella F. Bacon
Reception Date: Jan. 4, 1878
Removal Date: Jan. 1887
How removed: Died

~~~~~~~~~~~~~~~~~~

Line #: 19
Name: Rosamond D. Tower
Reception Date: Jan. 4, 1878
Removal Date: Aug. 29, 1897
How removed: Died

Line #: 20
Name: E. Mitchell Cole
Reception Date: Jan. 4, 1878
Removal Date: 1882
How removed: Died

~~~~~~~~~~~~~~~~~~

Line #: 21
Name: Alvin N. Lamb
Reception Date: Jan. 4, 1878
How received: Letter from Univ. Ch., Charlton, Mass.
Remarks: 15 Irving

~~~~~~~~~~~~~~~~~~

Line #: 22
Name: J. Louisa Lamb
Reception Date: Jan. 4, 1878
How received: Letter from Univ. Ch. Charlton, Mass.
Removal Date: Feb. 15, 1900
How removed: Died

~~~~~~~~~~~~~~~~~~

Line #: 23
Name: Van R. Kent
Reception Date: Jan. 5, 1879
Removal Date: Mar. 23, 1891
How removed: Transfered to St. Paul's Church, Denver, Col.

~~~~~~~~~~~~~~~~~~

Line #: 24
Name: Lelia Kent
Reception Date: Jan. 5, 1879
Removal Date: Mar 23, 1891
How removed: Transfered to St. Paul's Church, Denver, Col.

Line #: 25
Name: Alfred H. Johnson
Reception Date: Jan 7, 1881
Removal Date: Sept. 26, 1887
How removed: Died

~~~~~~~~~~~~~~~~~~

Line #: 26
Name: Anna S. Johnson
Reception Date: Jan 7, 1881
Remarks: 35 Cherry

~~~~~~~~~~~~~~~~~~

Line #: 27
Name: Vilroy Newton
Reception Date: Mar 25, 1883
Remarks: 34 Irving
Additional information from Book 2: Mrs. Vilroy Newton; Mrs. Chas. N.

~~~~~~~~~~~~~~~~~~

Line #: 28
Name: Emeline Slayton
Reception Date: Mar. 25, 1883
Remarks: Providence, R. I.
Additional information from Book 2: left town

~~~~~~~~~~~~~~~~~~

Line #: 29
Name: Frank A. Barr
Reception Date: Mar. 25, 1883
Remarks: Apr. 1909; Forest, Ohio, P. O. Box 404
Additional information from Book 2: left town

Line #: 30
Name: Seth D. Bradley
Reception Date: Mar 25, 1883
Remarks: Randolph, Mass.
Additional information from Book 2: left town

~~~~~~~~~~~~~~~~~~

Line #: 31
Name: Abbie B. Bradley
Reception Date: Mar. 25, 1883
Remarks: Middleboro—Mrs.
Additional information from Book 2: left town

~~~~~~~~~~~~~~~~~~

Line #: 32
Name: Lois B. Copp
Reception Date: Mar. 25, 1883
Remarks: 15 Irving

~~~~~~~~~~~~~~~~~~

Line #: 33
Name: Addie Desoe = Mrs. Bemis
Reception Date: Mar. 25, 1883
Removal Date: Mar. 30, 1899
How removed: Transfered to 1st Universalist Ch., Worcester, Mass.
Additional information from Book 2: left town

~~~~~~~~~~~~~~~~~~

Line #: 34
Name: Fannie Corbin
Reception Date: Mar 25, 1883
Remarks: 14 Holmes

~~~~~~~~~~~~~~~~~~

Line #: 35
Name: Nellie L. Stone-Prouty
Reception Date: Mar 25, 1883
Removal Date: Jul 23, 1907
How removed: Died July 23d 1907 in Hospital in Worcester. Funeral attended by F. A. Bisbee
Remarks: Mechanic
Additional information from Book 2: E. V. Prouty

~~~~~~~~~~~~~~~~~~

Line #: 36
Name: Cora J. Livermore-West
Reception Date: Mar. 25, 1883
Remarks: Newton, Mass.
Additional information from Book 2: Mrs. J. H. West; left town

~~~~~~~~~~~~~~~~~~

Line #: 37
Name: Fannie Bemis
Reception Date: Apr. 6, 1883
How removed: Died
Additional information from Book 2: Mrs. Fanny Bemis

~~~~~~~~~~~~~~~~~~

Line #: 38
Name: Edna Bemis-Procter
Reception Date: Apr 22, 1883
Remarks: Hillsville
Additional information from Book 2: Mrs. Proctor

~~~~~~~~~~~~~~~~~~

Line #: 39
Name: Ephrim G. Barr
Reception Date: Apr. 25, 1886
Removal Date: Dec. 1, 1909
How removed: Died

~~~~~~~~~~~~~~~~~~

Line #: 40
Name: Isaac L. Slayton
Reception Date: Apr. 25, 1886
Removal Date: June 1888
How removed: Died

~~~~~~~~~~~~~~~~~~

Line #: 41
Name: Edeith D. Bartholomew
Reception Date: Apr. 25, 1886
Remarks: Rev. J. G. wife of
Additional information from Book 2: Edith; left town

~~~~~~~~~~~~~~~~~~

Line #: 42
Name: Elnor J. Davis
Reception Date: Apr. 25, 1886
How removed: Transferred—Framingham 4/8, 1917
Remarks: 1851 N. Richmond St., Chicago, Ill.
Additional information from Book 2: Elinor; left town

~~~~~~~~~~~~~~~~~~

Line #: 43
Name: Effie M. Newton
Reception Date: Apr. 25, 1886
How removed: Died
Remarks: 34 Cherry

Line #: 44
Name: Lucy O. Newton
Reception Date: Apr. 25, 1886
Remarks: 34 Cherry

~~~~~~~~~~~~~~~~~~

Line #: 45
Name: Harriet M. Slayton-Valentine
Reception Date: Apr. 25, 1886
How received: Confirmed
Remarks: Boston
Additional information from Book 2: left town

~~~~~~~~~~~~~~~~~~

Line #: 46
Name: Mary J. Slayton
Reception Date: Apr. 25, 1886
Additional information from Book 2: left town

~~~~~~~~~~~~~~~~~~

Line #: 47
Name: Cora E. Leonard—Mrs. W.W. Taylor
Reception Date: Apr. 25, 1886
Remarks: 30 Beaumont St., Springfield

~~~~~~~~~~~~~~~~~~

Line #: 48
Name: Kattie M. Prouty-Capen
Reception Date: Apr. 25, 1886
Remarks: Main
Additional information from Book 2: Katie M. Prouty

Line #: 49
Name: Carrie M. Smith-Bemis
Reception Date: Apr. 25, 1886
Remarks: 43 Pleasant
Additional information from Book 2: Mrs. Lewis D. Bemis

~~~~~~~~~~~~~~~~~

Line #: 50
Name: Carrie L. Pierce-Goodrich
Reception Date: Apr. 25, 1886
Removal Date: Jul. 12, 1904
How removed: Transferred to Newtonville
Remarks: 287A Washington St., Newton, Mass.
Additional information from Book 2: left town

~~~~~~~~~~~~~~~~~

Line #: 51
Name: Minnie E. Draper-Burkill
Reception Date: Apr. 25, 1886
Remarks: Brookfield, Mass.; Mrs. Thomas Burkill
Additional information from Book 2: married to Burkill

~~~~~~~~~~~~~~~~~

Line #: 52
Name: Frances M. Pepper-Rice
Reception Date: Apr. 25, 1886
Remarks: Pleasant
Additional information from Book 2: Mrs. F. M. Rice; Cottage St.

~~~~~~~~~~~~~~~~~

Line #: 53
Name: Lucy J. Pepper
Reception Date: Apr 25, 1886
Removal Date: Mar. 17, 1889
How removed: Transferred to 1st Universalist Ch., Worcester, Mass.

~~~~~~~~~~~~~~~~~

Line #: 54
Name: Lizzie H. Amidon
Reception Date: Apr 25, 1886
Removal Date: June 30, 1899
How removed: Letter to 1st Congregational Ch., No. Brookfield, Mass.
Additional information from Book 2: Lizzie H. Amadon; left town; withdrawn

~~~~~~~~~~~~~~~~~

Line #: 55
Name: Jennie L. Worthington-Anderson
Reception Date: Apr 25, 1886
Remarks: Agawam
Additional information from Book 2: left town

~~~~~~~~~~~~~~~~~

Line #: 56
Name: Clara Bemis
Reception Date: Apr. 25, 1886
Removal Date: Mar. 17, 1889
How removed: Transfered to 1st Universalist Ch., Worcester, Mass.

~~~~~~~~~~~~~~~~~

Line #: 57
Name: Louise Mathews-Dennis, Married Loren J. D---
Reception Date: Apr. 10, 1887
Remarks: No. Adams, Mass.
Additional information from Book 2: Louise Matthews; left town

~~~~~~~~~~~~~~~~~~

Line #: 58
Name: Ida Howe-Mrs. John G. Prouty
Reception Date: Apr 10, 1887
Removal Date: April 2, 1909
How removed: Name dropped at her own request she having united with the Christian Scientists (see Appendix i)
Remarks: 25 High
Additional information from Book 2: Miss Ida Howe; Mrs. John Prouty

~~~~~~~~~~~~~~~~~~

Line #: 59
Name: Minnie Howe-Ross (Mrs. Willard D.)
Reception Date: Apr. 10, 1887
Removal Date: Sept. 14, 1906
How removed: Died Sept. 14, 1906

~~~~~~~~~~~~~~~~~~

Line #: 60
Name: Nellie Morse
Reception Date: Apr. 21, 1889
How received: Baptism
Remarks: 16 Irving

Additional information from Book 2: Mrs. Nellie Morse

~~~~~~~~~~~~~~~~~~

Line #: 61
Name: Emma Worthington
Reception Date: Apr. 21, 1889
How received: Baptism
Removal Date: May 3, 1890
How removed: Died
Additional information from Book 2: Mrs. Emma Worthington

~~~~~~~~~~~~~~~~~~

Line #: 62
Name: Mary Tabor
Reception Date: Jan. 5, 1890
How received: Baptism
Remarks: Cherry
Additional information from Book 2: Mrs. Mary Taber

~~~~~~~~~~~~~~~~~~

Line #: 63
Name: Alice I. Prouty
Reception Date: Jan. 5, 1890
How received: Baptism
Removal Date: Dec. 12, 1891
How removed: Died
Additional information from Book 2: Miss Alice I. Prouty

~~~~~~~~~~~~~~~~~~

Line #: 64
Name: Etta E. Sylvester
Reception Date: Jan. 5, 1890
How received: Baptism
Removal Date: Oct. 7, 1898

How removed: Transfered to
2nd Universalist Ch., Springfield,
Mass.
**Additional information from
Book 2:** Miss Etta E. Sylvester;
withdrawn

~~~~~~~~~~~~~~~~~

Line #: 65
Name: Annella Barr
Reception Date: Jan. 5, 1890
How received: Baptism
Remarks: 72 Pleasant
**Additional information from
Book 2:** Miss Annella Barr

~~~~~~~~~~~~~~~~~

Line #: 66
Name: W. W. Fay
Reception Date: Jan. 5, 1890
How received: Confession of
Faith
How removed: Died

~~~~~~~~~~~~~~~~~

Line #: 67
Name: Mrs. W. W. Fay
Reception Date: Jan. 5, 1890
How received: Confession of
Faith
Remarks: California

~~~~~~~~~~~~~~~~~

Line #: 68
Name: Mrs. Florence Pike
Reception Date: Jan. 5, 1890
How received: Letter From Univ.
Ch., Bath, Me.

Removal Date: May 25, 1892
How removed: Given Letter
**Additional information from
Book 2:** Granted letter of
dismissal and recommendation
May 25th 1892

~~~~~~~~~~~~~~~~~

Line #: 69
Name: Mary Etta Pike
Reception Date: Jan. 5, 1890
How received: Letter from
M[ethodist].E[picopal]. Ch.,
Ashland, Mass.
Removal Date: Sept. 1, 1903
How removed: Letter to
Charlton
**Additional information from
Book 2:** Mrs. Mary Etta Pike

~~~~~~~~~~~~~~~~~

Line #: 70
Name: Mrs. D. Corliss
Reception Date: Jan. 5, 1890
How received: Letter from Univ.
Ch.
Removal Date: July 1, 1893
How removed: Died

~~~~~~~~~~~~~~~~~

Line #: 71
Name: D. Corliss
Reception Date: Jan. 5, 1890
How received: Letter from Univ.
Ch.
Removal Date: Dec. 30, 1903
How removed: Died

~~~~~~~~~~~~~~~~~

Line #: 72
Name: Etta L. Prouty
Reception Date: Apr. 6, 1890
How received: Baptism
Removal Date: May 23, 1891
How removed: Died
**Additional information from
Book 2:** Miss Etta L. Prouty

~~~~~~~~~~~~~~~~~~

Line #: 73
Name: Sarah C. Wilder,
Carpenter
Reception Date: Apr. 6, 1890
How received: Baptism
Remarks: Boston—Wakefield

~~~~~~~~~~~~~~~~~~

Line #: 74
Name: Elmer S. Newton
Reception Date: Apr. 6, 1890
How received: Baptism
Remarks: Washington, D.C.

~~~~~~~~~~~~~~~~~~

Line #: 75
Name: Allan H. Faxon
Reception Date: Apr. 6, 1890
How received: Baptism
Remarks: Southbridge
**Additional information from
Book 2:** Transfered to
Southbridge Universalist Church;
left town

~~~~~~~~~~~~~~~~~~

Line #: 76
Name: Arthur R. Gledhill

Reception Date: Apr. 6, 1890
How received: Confirmation
Remarks: Plymouth
**Additional information from
Book 2:** left town

~~~~~~~~~~~~~~~~~~

Line #: 77
Name: Virginia Bourrett
Reception Date: April 6, 1890
How received: Letter from Univ
Ch., Woonsocket, RI
Remarks: Worcester

~~~~~~~~~~~~~~~~~~

Line #: 78
Name: Mrs. Sarah H. Jenks
Reception Date: Sept. 21, 1890
How received: Baptism
Remarks: Cincinnati
**Additional information from
Book 2:** Cincinnatti, O.; received
by baptism and con.

~~~~~~~~~~~~~~~~~~

Line #: 79
Name: Ida Warren
Reception Date: Jul. 30, 1893
How received: Letter from Univ
Ch., Roxbury, Mass.
Remarks: Leicester
**Additional information from
Book 2:** Mrs. Ida L. Warren

~~~~~~~~~~~~~~~~~~

Line #: 80
Name: Zylphia Fuller
Reception Date: Mar. 25, 1894

How received: Baptism
Remarks: Maine - Winthrop

~~~~~~~~~~~~~~~~~~~~

Line #: 81
Name: Edith Florence Howland-Bacon
Reception Date: Mar. 25, 1894
How received: Baptism
Remarks: Married Lewis H. Bacon = p. 112—36 Cherry

~~~~~~~~~~~~~~~~~~~~

Line #: 82
Name: Carrie Hunter Sibley-Saunders
Reception Date: Mar. 25, 1894
How received: Confirmation
Remarks: Residence Brookline

~~~~~~~~~~~~~~~~~~~~

Line #: 83
Name: Fannie Laura Bacon-Muzzy
Reception Date: Mar. 25, 1894
How received: Confirmation
Removal Date: Apr 8th, 1911
How removed: Letter of Transfer to All Souls, Worcester
Remarks: Married George D. Muzzy=p. 114; 44 Oread, Worcester

~~~~~~~~~~~~~~~~~~~~

Line #: 84
Name: E. Jennie Allen
Reception Date: Apr. 5, 1896

How received: Letter from All Souls Ch., Worcester, Mass.
Removal Date: Apr. 1, 1898
How removed: Transfered to Brookline Universalist Ch.
Additional information from Book 2: Miss E. Jennie Allen

~~~~~~~~~~~~~~~~~~~~

Line #: 85
Name: Della Tripp-Wetherbee (Learned)
Reception Date: Apr. 5, 1896
How received: Baptism
Remarks: 25 Mechanic
Additional information from Book 2: Mrs. Della Tripp Wetherbee

~~~~~~~~~~~~~~~~~~~~

Line #: 86
Name: Nellie Frances Edwards-Biscoe
Reception Date: Apr. 5, 1896
How received: Baptism
Remarks: So. of W. Main St.
Additional information from Book 2: Mrs. Nellie Frances Edwards

~~~~~~~~~~~~~~~~~~~~

Line #: 87
Name: Ella Frances Edwards-Cassavant
Reception Date: Apr. 5, 1896
How received: Confirmation
Remarks: Married Felix Cassavant, Jan. 1904

Line #: 88
Name: Elsia Gertrude Houghton
Reception Date: Apr. 5, 1896
How received: Baptism
How removed: Letter of Transfer to Hudson
Remarks: Hudson
Additional information from Book 2: Miss Elsie Gertrude Houghton

~~~~~~~~~~~~~~~~~~

Line #: 89
Name: Abner Pond
Reception Date: Apr. 5, 1896
How received: Baptism
How removed: Died

~~~~~~~~~~~~~~~~~~

Line #: 90
Name: Mrs. Mary Augusta Pond
Reception Date: Apr. 5, 1896
How received: Baptism
Removal Date: Dec. 30, 1899
How removed: Died

~~~~~~~~~~~~~~~~~~

Line #: 91
Name: Walter Edward Bellows
Reception Date: Apr. 5, 1896
How received: Baptism
Removal Date: June 27, 1909
How removed: Letter of Transfer to 1st Unitarian Church of Worcester

~~~~~~~~~~~~~~~~~~

Line #: 92
Name: Louisa Jane Bellows
Reception Date: Apr. 5, 1896
How received: Baptism
Remarks: Hudson
Additional information from Book 2: Miss Louisa Jane Bellows

~~~~~~~~~~~~~~~~~~

Line #: 93
Name: Alice Lucy Hoe Price
Reception Date: Apr. 5, 1896
How received: Confirmation
Remarks: Warren

~~~~~~~~~~~~~~~~~~

Line #: 94
Name: John Edward Bacon
Reception Date: Apr. 5, 1896
How received: Baptism
Removal Date: Feb. 4, 1898
How removed: Died

~~~~~~~~~~~~~~~~~~

Line #: 95
Name: Mary Jane Bacon
Reception Date: Apr. 5, 1896
How received: Baptism
Remarks: 36 Cherry
Additional information from Book 2: Mrs. Mary Jane Bacon

~~~~~~~~~~~~~~~~~~

Line #: 96
Name: Linus H. Bacon
Reception Date: Apr. 5, 1896
How received: Baptism

Remarks: Married=p.112; 36 Cherry

~~~~~~~~~~~~~~~~~~~

Line #: 97
Name: Mary Whitermore Warren Day
Reception Date: Apr. 5, 1896
How received: Confirmation
Removal Date: April 14, 1908
How removed: Letter of Transfer to Washington, D.C.
Remarks: Letter granted on instruction of Dea. Lamb & Pastor

~~~~~~~~~~~~~~~~~~~

Line #: 98
Name: Edna Henderson Johnson Austin
Reception Date: Apr. 5, 1896
How received: Confirmation
Removal Date: Apr. 10, 1908
How removed: Letter of Transfer to Pittsburg, Pa, April 10th 1908

~~~~~~~~~~~~~~~~~~~

Line #: 99
Name: Sarah H. Prouty
Reception Date: Apr. 5, 1896
How received: Baptism
Removal Date: Oct. 2, 1907
How removed: Died
Additional information from Book 2: Mrs. Sarah H. Prouty

~~~~~~~~~~~~~~~~~~~

Line #: 100
Name: Delia Mary Cobley
Reception Date: Apr. 5, 1896

How received: Baptism
Remarks: West Warren
Additional information from Book 2: Miss Delia Mary Cobley

~~~~~~~~~~~~~~~~~~~

Line #: 101
Name: Isaac L. Amidon
Reception Date: Apr. 5, 1896
How received: Baptism
Removal Date: Feb. 21, 1908
How removed: Died Feb. 21, 1908
Additional information from Book 2: left town

~~~~~~~~~~~~~~~~~~~

Line #: 102
Name: Chas. E. Hewett
Reception Date: Apr. 5, 1896
How received: Baptism
Remarks: New Bedford, Mass.
Additional information from Book 2: left town

~~~~~~~~~~~~~~~~~~~

Line #: 103
Name: Mrs. Chas. E. Hewett
Reception Date: Apr. 5, 1896
How received: Confirmation
Remarks: New Bedford, Mass.
Additional information from Book 2: left town

~~~~~~~~~~~~~~~~~~~

Line #: 104
Name: Mrs. Flint M. Bissell
Reception Date: Jan. 5, 1898

How received: Letter from Cambridge, Mass.
Removal Date: Mar. 30, 1899
How removed: Transferred to St. Pauls Ch., Springfield, Mass.

~~~~~~~~~~~~~~~~~

Line #: 105
Name: Miss Wilhelmina C. Hanscom
Reception Date: Jan. 5, 1898
How received: Letter from Cambridge, Mass.
Removal Date: Mar. 30, 1899
How removed: Transferred to St. Pauls Ch., Springfield, Mass.

~~~~~~~~~~~~~~~~~

Line #: 106
Name: Miss Rosella Addie Barton
Reception Date: Apr. 2, 1899
How received: Baptism
Removal Date: Aug. 28, 1908
How removed: Died
Remarks: 60 Cherry St.

~~~~~~~~~~~~~~~~~

Line #: 107
Name: Miss Lori Mae Trask/ Mrs. J. O. Mathews
Reception Date: Apr. 2, 1899
How received: Baptism
Remarks: 61 Lincoln

~~~~~~~~~~~~~~~~~

Line #: 108
Name: Miss Geraldine Stone Prouty

Reception Date: Apr. 2, 1899
How received: Baptism
How removed: Died
Remarks: Mechanic

~~~~~~~~~~~~~~~~~

Line #: 109
Name: Miss Ruth Anna Sibley
Reception Date: Apr. 2, 1899
How received: Confirmation
Remarks: 47 Cherry, Brookline

~~~~~~~~~~~~~~~~~

Line #: 110
Name: Miss Phebe Chandler Johnson/Mrs. Arthur E. Murdock
Reception Date: Apr 2, 1899
How received: Confirmation
Remarks: 35 Cherry; 455 Prospect Place, Brooklyn, NY

~~~~~~~~~~~~~~~~~

Line #: 111
Name: Miss Rhodicia Josephine Lovell
Reception Date: Apr. 2, 1899
How received: Confirmation
Remarks: 8 May

~~~~~~~~~~~~~~~~~

Line #: 112
Name: Miss Carrie Lydia Pond-Phillips
Reception Date: Apr. 2, 1899
How received: Confirmation
Remarks: Lynn

~~~~~~~~~~~~~~~~~

Line #: 113
Name: Miss Clara May Corliss
Reception Date: Apr. 2, 1899
How received: Confirmation
How removed: transferred to Lawrence
Remarks: 17 Lincoln, Lawrence, Mass.

~~~~~~~~~~~~~~~~~~

Line #: 114
Name: Mrs. Jennie M. Goodnow
Reception Date: Apr. 15, 1900
How received: Baptism
Remarks: 22 Holmes

~~~~~~~~~~~~~~~~~~

Line #: 115
Name: Miss Nellie A. Goodnow/Mrs. Boyden
Reception Date: Apr. 15, 1900
How received: Baptism
Remarks: Worcester

~~~~~~~~~~~~~~~~~~

Line #: 116
Name: Miss Josephine C. Goodnow
Reception Date: Apr. 15, 1900
How received: Baptism

~~~~~~~~~~~~~~~~~~

Line #: 117
Name: Miss Antine Goodnow-Mrs. Elton Prouty
Reception Date: Apr. 15, 1900
How received: Baptism

Remarks: Married Elton F. Prouty, Dec. 18,1907

~~~~~~~~~~~~~~~~~~

Line #: 118
Name: Miss Marion J. Jones-Lovell
Reception Date: Apr. 15, 1900
How received: Baptism
Remarks: Married to Chester Lovell; 8 May St.

~~~~~~~~~~~~~~~~~~

Line #: 119
Name: Miss Florence Ida Copp
Reception Date: Apr. 15, 1900
How received: Confirmation
Remarks: Married to Leigh E. Messer, Sept. 25, 1926; 15 Irving

~~~~~~~~~~~~~~~~~~

Line #: 120
Name: Mrs. Luella M. Masseck
Reception Date: Jul. 3, 1902
How received: Letter from N. Attleboro, Mass.
Removal Date: Apr. 30, 1905
How removed: Letter to Brattleboro, Vt.
Remarks: Arlington, Mass.

~~~~~~~~~~~~~~~~~~

Line #: 121
Name: Rev. Frank L. Masseck
Reception Date: Jul. 3, 1902
How received: Letter from N. Attleboro, Mass.
Removal Date: Apr 30, 1905

How removed: Letter to Brattleboro, Vt.
Remarks: Arlington, Mass.

~~~~~~~~~~~~~~~~~~

Line #: 122
Name: Miss Eleanor M. Davis— Mrs. Foster R. Wheeler
Reception Date: Jan. 4, 1903
How received: Confirmation
How removed: Letter to Framingham, 4/8, 1917
Remarks: 64 Rogers Ave., West Somerville, Mass.

~~~~~~~~~~~~~~~~~~

Line #: 123
Name: Roy F. Bingham
Reception Date: Mar. 31, 1904
How received: R. H. of F.
Removal Date: Apr. 12, 1905
How removed: Letter to Orange, Mass.
Remarks: P.O. Box 322, removed to Millers Falls, Mass.

~~~~~~~~~~~~~~~~~~

Line #: 124
Name: Fannie Elizabeth Proctor— Mrs. Robert Dwelley
Reception Date: Apr. 20, 1905
How received: R. H. of F.
How removed: died

~~~~~~~~~~~~~~~~~~

Line #: 125
Name: Mrs. Ellen A. Lamb
Reception Date: Jan. 2, 1909

How received: Baptism

~~~~~~~~~~~~~~~~~~

Line #: 126
Name: Mrs. Mary E. Bradley
Reception Date: Jan. 2, 1909
How received: R. H. of F. by Deacon A. N. Lamb
Remarks: Hinsdale, NH

~~~~~~~~~~~~~~~~~~

Line #: 127
Name: Rev. Asa M. Bradley
Reception Date: Jan. 2, 1909
How received: R. H. of F. by Deacon A. N. Lamb
Remarks: Called to Hinsdale, NH

~~~~~~~~~~~~~~~~~~

Line #: 128
Name: Mrs. Sarah A. Howe
Reception Date: Jan. 15, 1911
How received: Baptism

~~~~~~~~~~~~~~~~~~

Line #: 129
Name: Mrs. [blank] Bidwell
Reception Date: Apr. 16, 1911
How received: Baptism

~~~~~~~~~~~~~~~~~~

Line #: 130
Name: Mrs. Cyntha L. Hancock
Reception Date: Apr. 16, 1911
How received: Baptism

~~~~~~~~~~~~~~~~~~

Line #: 131
Name: Mr. Henry W. Warren
Reception Date: Apr. 16, 1911
How received: Confirmation
How removed: Letter
Remarks: Hartford, Conn.

~~~~~~~~~~~~~~~~~~~~~~

BAPTISM NOTES

~~~~~~~~~~~~~~~~~~~~~~

Information on the baptisms of members of the Universalist Church are located in Book 1, page 60-69. There are seven columns with the following headings: [line] number; names, in full; Christian names of parents; date of birth; date of baptism; date of confirmation, or admission to church on profession of faith; and remarks. Finally, we will include the additional information found only in Book 2, which lists Persons # 41-74 as being baptised by Rev. J. S. Gledhill. Not every column is filled in for each person. Also note that all information should be checked against other vital record sources as errors in the church records have been found; for example, the birth dates for the Lovell children.

Standardized punctuation was used. [ ] indicates words added by the editor. [ ] around data indicates a best guess as to what was written. The "Additions from Book 2" column includes, among other items, spelling variations.

The "Remarks" column sometimes included information on marriage or death, or was a place for including information on what appears to be forwarding addresses.

Dates were transcribed as they appeared in the original.

~~~~~~~~~~~~~~~~~~~~~~

BAPTISMS

~~~~~~~~~~~~~~~~~~~~~~

#: 1
Name: Lucia May Sumner
Date of Baptism: Sept. 30, 1877
Additions from Book 2: Died Sept. 30, 1877

~~~~~~~~~~~~~~~~~~

#: 2
Name: Geo. Francis Sumner
Date of Baptism: Sept. 30, 1877
Additions from Book 2:
Uxbridge 1882

~~~~~~~~~~~~~~~~~~

#: 3 (see Appendix ii)
Name: Jennie H. Sumner
Date of birth: June 2, 1868
Date of Baptism: Sept. 30, 1877
Additions from Book 2:
Uxbridge 1882

~~~~~~~~~~~~~~~~~~

#: 4
Name: Herbert Sumner
Date of Baptism: Sept. 30, 1877

Additions from Book 2:
Uxbridge 1882

~~~~~~~~~~~~~~~~~~~

#: 5
Name: Carrie Hunter Sibley
Christian Name of Parents:
Emory F. and Mary P. Bullard
Date of birth: April 11, 1875
Date of Baptism: June 22, 1879
**Date of Confirmation or
Admission to Church on
Profession of Faith:** Mar. 25,
1894
Remarks: Married Dr. Saunders
1903

~~~~~~~~~~~~~~~~~~~

#: 6
Name: Fannie Laura Bacon
Christian Name of Parents:
Arthur B. and Ella Kent
Date of birth: Oct. 5, 1876
Date of Baptism: June 22, 1879
**Date of Confirmation or
Admission to Church on
Profession of Faith:** Mar. 25,
1894
Remarks: Married Geo. Muzzy
1902

~~~~~~~~~~~~~~~~~~~

#: 7
Name: Fred Kent Bacon
Christian Name of Parents:
Arthur B. and Ella Kent
Date of Baptism: June 22, 1879
Remarks: Died Dec. 7, 1901

#: 8
Name: Arthur Minott Warren
Christian Name of Parents:
[blank] and [blank]
Date of Baptism: June 22, 1879
Remarks: Worcester
Additions from Book 2: left
town

~~~~~~~~~~~~~~~~~~~

#: 9
Name: Wells Everett Lackey
Date of Baptism: June 22, 1879
Additions from Book 2: left
town

~~~~~~~~~~~~~~~~~~~

#: 10
Name: Samm Everett Adams
Date of Baptism: June 22, 1879
Additions from Book 2: left
town

~~~~~~~~~~~~~~~~~~~

#: 11
Name: Elbert Lee Wilson
Christian Name of Parents:
Oscar and Lydia B.
Date of Baptism: June 22, 1879
Additions from Book 2: son
O.W.W.

~~~~~~~~~~~~~~~~~~~

#: 12
Name: Geo. Adison Drury
Date of Baptism: (out) June 19,
1881

Additions from Book 2: lives in Boston

~~~~~~~~~~~~~~~~~

#: 13
Name: Joseph Slayton
Date of Baptism: June 19, 1881
Remarks: Died

~~~~~~~~~~~~~~~~~

#: 14
Name: Elmer Newton
Christian Name of Parents: Chas. and Vilroy S.
Date of Baptism: June 19, 1881
Date of Confirmation or Admission to Church on Profession of Faith: April 6, 1890
Remarks: Washington DC

~~~~~~~~~~~~~~~~~

#: 15
Name: Edile H. Clark
Christian Name of Parents: Hiram and Lottie Hale
Date of birth: Mar. 16, 1874
Date of Baptism: June 19, 1881
Remarks: Brookfield
Additions from Book 2: Boston Branch Grocery

~~~~~~~~~~~~~~~~~

#: 16
Name: Edna Bemis
Date of Baptism: June 19, 1881
Additions from Book 2: Proctor
~~~~~~~~~~~~~~~~~

#: 17
Name: Clara Robinson
Date of Baptism: June 19, 1881
Remarks: Married Wm. A. Mills. Removed to Chicago. Killed in Iroquois Theater disaster, Chicago, Dec. 30, 1903 [see Appendix vi]
Additions from Book 2: left town

~~~~~~~~~~~~~~~~~

#: 18
Name: Angie Putnam
Christian Name of Parents: Elija and Mary S.
Date of Baptism: June 19, 1881
Additions from Book 2: left town

~~~~~~~~~~~~~~~~~

#: 19
Name: Mary J. Slayton
Christian Name of Parents: Isaac and Emeline
Date of Baptism: June 19, 1881
Date of Confirmation or Admission to Church on Profession of Faith: April 25, 1886
Additions from Book 2: left town

~~~~~~~~~~~~~~~~~

#: 20
Name: Marion L. Kent
Christian Name of Parents: Van R. and Lelia Foster
Date of Baptism: June 19, 1881

Remarks: Colorado
Additions from Book 2: Denver

~~~~~~~~~~~~~~~~~~

#: 21
Name: Edna Henderson Johnson
Christian Name of Parents:
Alfred H. and Annie Bullard
Date of birth: Sept. 30, 1878
Date of Baptism: June 19, 1881
**Date of Confirmation or
Admission to Church on
Profession of Faith:** April 5,
1896
Remarks: Married Sept. 15, 1906
to Wm. W. Austin, Pittsburg, Pa.

~~~~~~~~~~~~~~~~~~

#: 22
Name: Edgar Bemis
Date of Baptism: June 25, 1882
Additions from Book 2:
Grandson to Joshua Bemis

~~~~~~~~~~~~~~~~~~

#: 23
Name: Emma A. Gibson
Date of Baptism: June 25, 1882

~~~~~~~~~~~~~~~~~~

#: 24
Name: Robert Gibson
Date of Baptism: June 25, 1882

~~~~~~~~~~~~~~~~~~

#: 25
Name: Chas. D. Hobbs

Christian Name of Parents:
Samuel D. and [blank]
Date of Baptism: June 25, 1882

~~~~~~~~~~~~~~~~~~

#: 26
Name: Chas. Edward Lackey
Date of Baptism: June 25, 1882
Additions from Book 2: Milford

~~~~~~~~~~~~~~~~~~

#: 27
Name: Ralph Kent
Christian Name of Parents: Van
R. and Lelia Foster
Date of birth: 1882
Date of Baptism: June 1884

~~~~~~~~~~~~~~~~~~

#: 28
Name: Phebe Chandler Johnson
Christian Name of Parents:
Alfred H. and Annie Bullard
Date of birth: June 9, 1884
Date of Baptism: June 1884 ["4"
crossed out and replaced with a
"6"]
**Date of Confirmation or
Admission to Church on
Profession of Faith:** April 2,
1899

~~~~~~~~~~~~~~~~~~

#: 29
Name: Ruth Anna Sibley
Christian Name of Parents:
Emory F. and Mary Bullard
Date of birth: March 30, 1883
Date of Baptism: June 1884

Date of Confirmation or Admission to Church on Profession of Faith: April 2, 1899

~~~~~~~~~~~~~~~~~~

#: 30
Name: Fred Robinson
Date of Baptism: June 1884

~~~~~~~~~~~~~~~~~~

#: 31
Name: Nina Eaton
Date of Baptism: June 1884
Additions from Book 2: left town

~~~~~~~~~~~~~~~~~~

#: 32
Name: Ella Louisa Bacon
Christian Name of Parents: Arthur B. and Ella Kent
Date of birth: Jan. 1, 1883
Date of Baptism: June 1884
Remarks: Died 1886
Additions from Book 2: Ella Louise Bacon

~~~~~~~~~~~~~~~~~~

#: 33
Name: Ethen Hammond Lovell
Christian Name of Parents: Ethen H. and Anna Cross
Date of birth: Oct. 16, 1888 [sic 1880]
Date of Baptism: June 1886
Additions from Book 2: Ethan Hammond Lovell

#: 34
Name: Chester Cross Lovell
Christian Name of Parents: Ethen H. and Anna Cross
Date of birth: Sept. 5, 1883 [sic 1882]
Date of Baptism: June 1886

~~~~~~~~~~~~~~~~~~

#: 35
Name: Rhodicia Josephine Lovell
Christian Name of Parents: Ethen H. and Anna Cross
Date of birth: Jan. 1, 1885
Date of Baptism: June 1886
Date of Confirmation or Admission to Church on Profession of Faith: April 2, 1899

~~~~~~~~~~~~~~~~~~

#: 36
Name: [blank] Wilson
Date of Baptism: June 1886

~~~~~~~~~~~~~~~~~~

#: 37
Name: Amy Josephine Bemis
Date of Baptism: 1887

~~~~~~~~~~~~~~~~~~

#: 38
Name: [blank] Desoe
Date of Baptism: 1887

~~~~~~~~~~~~~~~~~~

#: 39
Name: [blank] Corliss
Date of Baptism: 1887

~~~~~~~~~~~~~~~~~~

#: 40
Name: [blank] Barr
Date of Baptism: 1887

~~~~~~~~~~~~~~~~~~

#: 41
Name: Lula May Grout
Date of Baptism: June 9, 1889

~~~~~~~~~~~~~~~~~~

#: 42
Name: Florence Lucinda Wilson
Date of Baptism: June 9, 1889

~~~~~~~~~~~~~~~~~~

#: 43
Name: Flo[nn]ie May Prouty
Christian Name of Parents:
Frank and Belle K.
Date of birth: Sept. 4, 1883
Date of Baptism: June 9, 1889

~~~~~~~~~~~~~~~~~~

#: 44
Name: Iva Grace Putnam
Date of Baptism: June 9, 1889
~~~~~~~~~~~~~~~~~~

#: 45
Name: Suanna Cynthia
Worthington
Date of Baptism: June 9, 1889

#: 46
Name: Arthur Henry Copp
Christian Name of Parents:
Henry and Lois Lamb
Date of birth: Feb. 14, 1884
Date of Baptism: June 9, 1889

~~~~~~~~~~~~~~~~~~

sophia
#: 47
Name: Oscar Mellan Howland
Christian Name of Parents: E.
Harris and Sarah Mellen
Date of Baptism: June 9, 1889

~~~~~~~~~~~~~~~~~~

#: 48
Name: Dale Carlton Hoe
Date of Baptism: June 9, 1889

~~~~~~~~~~~~~~~~~~

#: 49
Name: Blanch Ethel Tabor
Christian Name of Parents:
Edward and Mary
Date of Baptism: June 9, 1889
Additions from Book 2: Blanche
Ethel Taber

~~~~~~~~~~~~~~~~~~

#: 50
Name: Jennie Adeline Trembley
Christian Name of Parents:
Joseph and Anna Bemis
Date of Baptism: June 9, 1889
Remarks: Died Sept. 13 1899

~~~~~~~~~~~~~~~~~~

#: 51
Name: Alice Lucy Hoe
Date of Baptism: June 9, 1889
Date of Confirmation or Admission to Church on Profession of Faith: April 5, 1896

~~~~~~~~~~~~~~~~~~

#: 52
Name: Florence Maynard
Date of Baptism: June 9, 1889

~~~~~~~~~~~~~~~~~~

#: 53
Name: Josie Maria Wilson
Christian Name of Parents: Waldo and Amelia B.
Date of Baptism: June 9, 1889

~~~~~~~~~~~~~~~~~~

#: 54
Name: Julius Russel Sibley
Christian Name of Parents: Paul and Virginia A.
Date of Baptism: June 9, 1889

~~~~~~~~~~~~~~~~~~

#: [55]
Name: Elmer Fredrick Edwards
Date of Baptism: June 9, 1889
Additions from Book 2: Elmer Frederick Edwards

~~~~~~~~~~~~~~~~~~

#: [56]
Name: Earnest Fay Edwards
Date of Baptism: June 9, 1889

~~~~~~~~~~~~~~~~~~

#: [57]
Name: Carrie Lydia Pond
Christian Name of Parents: Abner and Mary
Date of Baptism: June 9, 1889
Date of Confirmation or Admission to Church on Profession of Faith: April 2, 1899

~~~~~~~~~~~~~~~~~~

#: [58]
Name: Marian Maynard
Date of Baptism: June 9, 1889
Additions from Book 2: Marion Maynard

~~~~~~~~~~~~~~~~~~

#: [59]
Name: Frank Hastings Hammond
Date of Baptism: June 9, 1889

~~~~~~~~~~~~~~~~~~

#: [60]
Name: Florence Ida Copp
Christian Name of Parents: Henry and Lois Lamb
Date of birth: Oct. 24, 1885
Date of Baptism: June 9, 1889
Date of Confirmation or Admission to Church on Profession of Faith: April 15, 1900

~~~~~~~~~~~~~~~~~~

#: [61]
Name: Miriam Elsie Lamb
Christian Name of Parents: Geo.
and Sada Drury
Date of birth: Jan. 8, 1889
Date of Baptism: June 9, 1889

~~~~~~~~~~~~~~~~~~

#: [62]
Name: Alice Louise Bemis
Christian Name of Parents:
Louis and [blank]
Date of Baptism: June 9, 1889

~~~~~~~~~~~~~~~~~~

#: [63]
Name: Harold Franklin Desoe
Christian Name of Parents:
Edward and Nettie Drury
Date of Baptism: June 9, 1889

~~~~~~~~~~~~~~~~~~

#: [64]
Name: George Fredrick Parker
Date of Baptism: June 8, 1890

~~~~~~~~~~~~~~~~~~

#: [65]
Name: Clifton Adelbert Parker
Date of Baptism: June 8, 1890

~~~~~~~~~~~~~~~~~~

#: [66]
Name: Sarah Ethel Parker
Date of Baptism: June 8, 1890

~~~~~~~~~~~~~~~~~~

#: [67]
Name: Nettie Florence Tabor
Christian Name of Parents:
Edward and Mary
Date of Baptism: June 8, 1890
Additions from Book 2: Nettie
Florence Taber

~~~~~~~~~~~~~~~~~~

#: [68]
Name: Alice May Hoar
Date of Baptism: June 8, 1890
Remarks: Worcester

~~~~~~~~~~~~~~~~~~

#: [69]
Name: Earl Frank Rice
Christian Name of Parents:
Frank and Frances Pepper
Date of Baptism: June 14, 1891

~~~~~~~~~~~~~~~~~~

#: [70]
Name: Myron Wesley Bemis
Christian Name of Parents:
Louis and [blank]
Date of Baptism: June 14, 1891
~~~~~~~~~~~~~~~~~~

#: [71]
Name: Robert Lippitt Warren
Christian Name of Parents:
Edward and Ida Lippitt
Date of Baptism: June 14, 1891

~~~~~~~~~~~~~~~~~~

#: [72]
Name: Henry Wheeler Warren
Christian Name of Parents:
Edward and Ida Lippitt
Date of Baptism: June 14, 1891
**Date of Confirmation or
Admission to Church on
Profession of Faith:** April 16,
1911

~~~~~~~~~~~~~~~~~~

#: [73]
Name: Rachel Catherine Warren
Christian Name of Parents:
Edward and Ida Lippitt
Date of Baptism: June 14, 1891

~~~~~~~~~~~~~~~~~~

#: [74]
Name: Mary Whitermore Warren
Christian Name of Parents:
Edward and Ida Lippitt
Date of Baptism: June 14, 1891
**Date of Confirmation or
Admission to Church on
Profession of Faith:** April 5,
1896
Additions from Book 2: Mary
Whittemore Warren

~~~~~~~~~~~~~~~~~~

#: 74a
Name: Zylphia Fuller
Date of Baptism: March 25,
1894
Additions from Book 2: found
in Book 2 only

~~~~~~~~~~~~~~~~~~

#: 74b
Name: Edith Florence Howland
Date of Baptism: March 25,
1894
Additions from Book 2: found
in Book 2 only

~~~~~~~~~~~~~~~~~~

#: [75]
Name: Bertha Marjorie Warren
Christian Name of Parents:
Edward and Ida Lippitt
Date of Baptism: June 17, 1894

~~~~~~~~~~~~~~~~~~

#: [76]
Name: Edward Irving Warren
Christian Name of Parents:
Edward and Ida Lippitt
Date of Baptism: June 17, 1894
Additions from Book 2: Edward
Erving Warren

~~~~~~~~~~~~~~~~~~

#: [77]
Name: Jennie Eldora Fuller
Christian Name of Parents: Geo.
and Zilphia
Date of Baptism: June 17, 1894

~~~~~~~~~~~~~~~~~~

#: [78]
Name: Harlo Murch Fuller
Christian Name of Parents: Geo
and Zilphia
Date of Baptism: June 17, 1894

~~~~~~~~~~~~~~~~~~

#: [79]
Name: Ruth Hathaway
Christian Name of Parents:
William and Cora Wilson
Date of birth: Jan. 15, 1893
Date of Baptism: June 9, 1895

~~~~~~~~~~~~~~~~~~~

#: [80]
Name: Walter Franklin Pratt
Christian Name of Parents:
Joshia P. and Emma
Date of birth: May 6, 1893
Date of Baptism: June 9, 1895
Additions from Book 2: Parents
Josiah Palmer & Emma

~~~~~~~~~~~~~~~~~~

#: 81
Name: John Alfred Corliss
Christian Name of Parents:
Dennison and Christiana
Date of birth: April 27, 1887
Date of Baptism: June 9, 1895
Additions from Book 2: Parents
Dennison F. & Christiana

~~~~~~~~~~~~~~~~~~~

#: [82]
Name: Bessie Leah Valentine
Christian Name of Parents:
James and Hattie Slayton
Date of birth: Oct. 30, 1888
Date of Baptism: June 9, 1895
Additions from Book 2: Parents
Jas. D. & Hattie M.

~~~~~~~~~~~~~~~~~~~

#: [83]
Name: Edward Hudson Brigham
Christian Name of Parents:
Fred and Mary White
Date of birth: May 15, 1885
Date of Baptism: June 9, 1895
Additions from Book 2: Edword
Hudson Brigham; Parents Fred
Austin & Mary Ellen

~~~~~~~~~~~~~~~~~~~

#: [84]
Name: Irving Ray Wilson
Christian Name of Parents:
Oscar and Lydia Bemis
Date of birth: Aug. 16, 1893
Date of Baptism: June 9, 1895
Additions from Book 2: Parents
Oscar W. & Lydia A.

~~~~~~~~~~~~~~~~~~

#: [85]
Name: Orin Gilbert Fuller
Christian Name of Parents: Geo.
and Zilphia
Date of birth: July 11, 1889
Date of Baptism: June 9, 1895
Additions from Book 2: Parents
Geo. N. & Zilphia

~~~~~~~~~~~~~~~~~~

#: [86]
Name: Margerett Adeline Prouty
Christian Name of Parents:
Frank and Sarah Howe
Date of birth: Sept. 1, 1891
Date of Baptism: June 9, 1895

Additions from Book 2: Parents
Frank I. & Sarah

~~~~~~~~~~~~~~~~~~~

#: [87]
Name: Mable Frances White
Christian Name of Parents:
Joseph and Nellie Green
Date of birth: Aug. 13, 1887
Date of Baptism: June 9, 1895
Additions from Book 2: Mabel
Frances White; Parents Joseph G.
& Nellie L.

~~~~~~~~~~~~~~~~~~~

#: [88]
Name: Fannie E. Procter
Christian Name of Parents:
Henry and Edna Bemis
Date of birth: Aug. 20, 1888
Date of Baptism: June 9, 1895
Additions from Book 2: Parents
Henry H. & Edna F.

~~~~~~~~~~~~~~~~~~~

#: [89]
Name: Harry E. Procter
Christian Name of Parents:
Henry and Edna Bemis
Date of birth: May 27, 1891
Date of Baptism: June 9, 1895

~~~~~~~~~~~~~~~~~~~

#: [90]
Name: Alfred Howe Prouty
Christian Name of Parents:
John and Ida Howe
Date of birth: 1895

Date of Baptism: June 14, 1896
Additions from Book 2: 9 mos.
old; Parents John G. Prouty & Ida
Howe Prouty

~~~~~~~~~~~~~~~~~~~

#: [91]
Name: Myron Cecil White
Christian Name of Parents:
Joseph and Nellie Green
Date of birth: July 29, 1894
Date of Baptism: June 14, 1896
Additions from Book 2: Parents
Joseph Gallup White & Nellie
Lydia White

~~~~~~~~~~~~~~~~~~~

#: [92]
Name: Alice May Abbott
Christian Name of Parents:
Frank and May
Date of Baptism: June 14, 1896
Additions from Book 2: about 3
yrs. old

~~~~~~~~~~~~~~~~~~~

#: [93]
Name: Marion Marvin
Christian Name of Parents:
Thomas and Flora Sugden
Date of Baptism: May 23, 1897
Remarks: Baptised by her father
Thomas A. Marvin

~~~~~~~~~~~~~~~~~~~

#: [94]
Name: Lloid Dennison Hunter

Christian Name of Parents:
[blank] and Lydia Corliss
Date of Baptism: June 20, 1897
Additions from Book 2: Lloyd
Dennison Hunter

~~~~~~~~~~~~~~~~~

#: [95]
Name: George Waterville Sibley
Christian Name of Parents: C. J.
[blank] Sibley
Date of Baptism: June 20, 1897

~~~~~~~~~~~~~~~~~

#: [96]
Name: Fredrick Chiron Sibley
Christian Name of Parents: C. J.
[blank] Sibley
Date of Baptism: June 20, 1897

~~~~~~~~~~~~~~~~~

#: [97]
Name: Carrie Louisa Sibley
Christian Name of Parents: C. J.
[blank] Sibley
Date of Baptism: June 20, 1897

~~~~~~~~~~~~~~~~~

#: [98]
Name: Minna Edith Burns
Date of Baptism: June 20, 1897
Additions from Book 2: Minnie
Edith Burns

~~~~~~~~~~~~~~~~~

#: [99]
Name: Walter Bowen Burnes

Date of Baptism: June 20, 1897
Additions from Book 2: Walter
Bowen Burns

~~~~~~~~~~~~~~~~~

#: [100]
Name: Sabin Alfred Morse
Christian Name of Parents:
Edward and Jennie G.
Date of Baptism: June 20, 1897

~~~~~~~~~~~~~~~~~

#: [101]
Name: Anna Christine Warren
Christian Name of Parents:
Edward and Ida Lippitt
Date of Baptism: June 12, 1898

~~~~~~~~~~~~~~~~~

#: [102]
Name: Frank Wilson Hathaway
Christian Name of Parents:
William and Cora Wilson
Date of Baptism: June 12, 1898
Additions from Book 2:
[Parent:] W. H. Hathaway

~~~~~~~~~~~~~~~~~

#: [103]
Name: Harold Belcher Barr
Christian Name of Parents:
Alton and Nettie Belcher
Date of Baptism: June 12, 1898
Additions from Book 2:
[Parent:] A. H. Barr

~~~~~~~~~~~~~~~~~

#: [104]
Name: Beatrice Page
Date of birth: Sept. 24, 1896
Date of Baptism: June 12, 1898
Additions from Book 2:
[Parent:] J. L. Page

~~~~~~~~~~~~~~~~~~

#: [105]
Name: Eliza May Bemis
Christian Name of Parents:
Louis and Carrie Smith
Date of birth: March 16, 1896
Date of Baptism: June 12, 1898
Additions from Book 2:
[Parent:] L. D. Bemis

~~~~~~~~~~~~~~~~~~

#: [106]
Name: Edward Oscar Wilson
Christian Name of Parents:
Oscar W. and Lydia A. Bemis
Date of birth: May 14, 1898
Date of Baptism: June 18, 1899

~~~~~~~~~~~~~~~~~~

#: [107]
Name: Edeith Ellen Hazelhurst
Christian Name of Parents:
Frank C. & Nellie E. Hatstat
Date of birth: Sept. 20, 1898
Date of Baptism: June 18, 1899

~~~~~~~~~~~~~~~~~~

#: 108
Name: Ethelyn Seraph Bemis
Christian Name of Parents:
Lewis D. & Carrie Smith

Date of birth: May 4, 1898
Date of Baptism: June 18, 1899

~~~~~~~~~~~~~~~~~~

#: 109
Name: Gertrude Louisa Bacon
Christian Name of Parents:
William E. and S. Antonnette
[Carpenter]
Date of birth: Jan. 22, 1899
Date of Baptism: June 18, 1899

~~~~~~~~~~~~~~~~~~

#: 110
Name: Ruth Margrette Trask
Date of birth: Feb. 19, 1896
Date of Baptism: June 17, 1900

~~~~~~~~~~~~~~~~~~

#: 111
Name: Rachel Bacon
Christian Name of Parents:
Linus H. and Edith F. Howland
Date of Baptism: June 16, 1901

~~~~~~~~~~~~~~~~~~

#: 112
Name: George Richard Prouty
Christian Name of Parents:
John G. and Ida Howe
Date of Baptism: June 8, 1902
Remarks: Frank Lincoln
Masseck, Minister

~~~~~~~~~~~~~~~~~~

#: 113
Name: Arthur Rudolph Prouty

Christian Name of Parents:
John G. and Ida Howe
Date of Baptism: June 8, 1902
Remarks: Frank Lincoln
Masseck, Minister

~~~~~~~~~~~~~~~~~~

#: 114
Name: Elsie Miriam Proctor
Christian Name of Parents:
Henry H. and Edna Bemis
Date of Baptism: June 8, 1902
Remarks: Frank Lincoln
Masseck, Minister

~~~~~~~~~~~~~~~~~~

#: 115
Name: Martha Bemis Proctor
Christian Name of Parents:
Henry H. and Edna Bemis
Date of Baptism: June 8, 1902
Remarks: Frank Lincoln
Masseck, Minister

~~~~~~~~~~~~~~~~~~

#: 116
Name: Everett Edwin Rice
Christian Name of Parents:
Frank E. and Francis M. Rice
Date of Baptism: June 14, 1903
Remarks: Frank Lincoln
Masseck, Minister

~~~~~~~~~~~~~~~~~~

#: 117
Name: Mary Bacon
Christian Name of Parents:
Linus H. and Edith F. Bacon

Date of Baptism: June 14, 1903
Remarks: Frank Lincoln
Masseck, Minister

~~~~~~~~~~~~~~~~~~

#: 118
Name: Mary Pond Beers
Christian Name of Parents:
[blank] and Nellie J. Beers
Date of Baptism: June 14, 1903
Remarks: Frank Lincoln
Masseck, Minister

~~~~~~~~~~~~~~~~~~

#: 119
Name: Alfred Prouty Capen
Christian Name of Parents:
Hubert H. and Kate M. Capen
Date of Baptism: June 14, 1903
Remarks: Frank Lincoln
Masseck, Minister

~~~~~~~~~~~~~~~~~~

#: 120
Name: Jennie Francis Rice
Christian Name of Parents:
Frank E. and Francis M. Rice
Date of Baptism: June 12, 1904
Remarks: Frank Lincoln
Masseck, Minister

~~~~~~~~~~~~~~~~~~

#: 121
Name: Hersey Elton Corser
Christian Name of Parents:
Edgar and [blank] Corser
Date of Baptism: June 12, 1904
Remarks: Frank Lincoln
Masseck, Minister

#: 122
Name: Alva Clara Corser
Christian Name of Parents:
Edgar and [blank] Corser
Date of Baptism: June 12, 1904
Remarks: Frank Lincoln
Masseck, Minister

~~~~~~~~~~~~~~~~~~

#: 123
Name: Eleanor Louise Warren
Christian Name of Parents:
Edward and Ida L. Warren
Date of birth: June 4, 1901
Date of Baptism: June 10, 1906

~~~~~~~~~~~~~~~~~~

#: 124
Name: Raymond Kenneth Rice
Christian Name of Parents:
Frank E. and Frances Rice
Date of birth: Mar. 10, 1905
Date of Baptism: June 9, 1907

~~~~~~~~~~~~~~~~~~

#: 125
Name: Eugene Earnest Bunnell
Christian Name of Parents:
Wm. Robert and Margaret
Melissa Bunnell
Date of birth: April 24, 1901
Date of Baptism: June 14, 1908

~~~~~~~~~~~~~~~~~~

#: 126
Name: Josephine Minerva
Boyden

Christian Name of Parents: Geo
E. and Nellie A. Goodnow
Date of birth: July 31, 1908
Date of Baptism: June 13, 1909

~~~~~~~~~~~~~~~~~~

#: 127
Name: Gladys Ella Barr
Christian Name of Parents:
Alton H. and Mary Lois
Date of birth: Dec. 30, 1908
Date of Baptism: June 13, 1909

~~~~~~~~~~~~~~~~~~

#: 127a
Name: Richard Paige Slayton
Christian Name of Parents:
Frank Herbert & Louise Mabel
Slayton
Date of birth: Aug. 7, 1909
Date of Baptism: June 18, 1911
Additions from Book 2: [found
on loose piece of paper]

~~~~~~~~~~~~~~~~~~

#: 127b
Name: Elizabeth Hadley Austin
Christian Name of Parents:
William Willis & Edna Henderson
Austin
Date of birth: July 18, 1910
Date of Baptism: June 18, 1911
Additions from Book 2: [found
on loose piece of paper]

~~~~~~~~~~~~~~~~~~

#: 127c
Name: Ruth Evelyn Boyden

Christian Name of Parents:
George Emerson & Nellie Agusta
Boyden
Date of birth: Feb. 1, 1910
Date of Baptism: June 18, 1911
Additions from Book 2: [found
on loose piece of paper]

~~~~~~~~~~~~~~~~~~~~

#: 127d
Name: Marion Alice Sibley
Christian Name of Parents:
Walter Edward & Alice May
Sibley
Date of birth: Aug. 17, 1909
Date of Baptism: June 18, 1911
Additions from Book 2: [found
on loose piece of paper]

~~~~~~~~~~~~~~~~~~~~

#: 127e
Name: Foster Russell Bemis
Christian Name of Parents:
Frank R. & Mary J. Bemis
Date of birth: Sept. 11, 1906
Date of Baptism: June 18, 1911
Additions from Book 2: [found
on loose piece of paper]

~~~~~~~~~~~~~~~~~~~~

#: 127f
Name: Stuart Otis Bemis
Christian Name of Parents:
Frank R. & Mary J. Bemis
Date of birth: Aug. 20, 1909
Date of Baptism: June 18, 1911
Additions from Book 2: [found
on loose piece of paper]

~~~~~~~~~~~~~~~~~~~~

~~~~~~~~~~~~~~~~~~~~~~~
MARRIAGE NOTES
~~~~~~~~~~~~~~~~~~~~~~~

Information on the marriages of
members of the Universalist
Church are located in Book 1,
page 100-121. There are two
rows, one for **Groom** and one for
Bride, made up of twelve
columns with the following
headings: no. (as nothing is
written in this column, page
number has been substituted
instead); name; age; occupation;
birthplace; father's name;
mother's (maiden) name; place;
date; officiating clergy; no. of
marriage; and witnesses. Finally,
we will include the additional
information found only in Book 2.
Not every column is filled in for
each person.

Standardized punctuation was
used. [ ] indicates words added
by the editor. [ ] around data
indicates a best guess as to what
was written. The "Additions from
Book 2" column includes spelling
variations as well as a date
discrepancy.

Dates were transcribed as they
appeared in the original.

~~~~~~~~~~~~~~~~~~~~~~~
MARRIAGES
~~~~~~~~~~~~~~~~~~~~~~~

Page: 100-101
Groom Name: Lewis F. White

Occupation: Farmer
Birth Place: Charlton, Mass
Father: Chas.
Mother: Charlotte ---
Number of marriage: 1
Bride Name: Isabel F. Miller
Father: F.X.
Number of marriage: 1
Wedding Place: Bride 's House, Spencer
Date: Nov. 22, 1877
Clergy: F. A. Bisbee

~~~~~~~~~~~~~~~~~~

Page: 100-101
Groom Name: Henry P. Howland
Occupation: [Spice?]dealer
Birth Place: Spencer, Mass.
Father: Pardon
Number of marriage: 1
Bride Name: Clara L. Bush
Birth Place: Spencer, Mass.
Father: John L.
Mother: Elinor Grout
Number of marriage: 1
Wedding Place: Spencer, Mass.
Date: Nov. 28, 1877
Clergy: F. A. Bisbee

~~~~~~~~~~~~~~~~~~

Page: 100-101
Groom Name: Chas. H. Green
Occupation: Boot Manufacturer
Birth Place: Spencer, Mass.
Father: Henry R.
Number of marriage: 1
Bride Name: Ella Converse
Birth Place: Spencer, Mass.
Father: Sibley Dexter
Number of marriage: 1

Wedding Place: Spencer, Mass.
Date: Dec. 1877
Clergy: F. A. Bisbee

~~~~~~~~~~~~~~~~~~

Page: 100-101
Groom Name: Alfred H. Johnson
Occupation: Printer
Birth Place: Tenn.
Number of marriage: 1
Bride Name: Anna S. Bullard
Birth Place: Spencer
Father: Dexter
Mother: Sophia Clapp
Number of marriage: 1
Wedding Place: Spencer, Mass.
Date: Dec. 25, 1877
Clergy: F. A. Bisbee
Variations in Book 2: Annie S. Bullard

~~~~~~~~~~~~~~~~~~

Page: 100-101
Groom Name: Marshall D. Barr
Bride Name: Mira Watson
Wedding Date: Jan. 1, 1878
Clergy: F. A. Bisbee

~~~~~~~~~~~~~~~~~~

Page: 100-101
Groom Name: Chas. H. Sibley
Bride Name: Grace G. Lackey
Wedding Date: Nov. 27, 1879
Clergy: F. A. Bisbee

~~~~~~~~~~~~~~~~~~

Page: 100-101
Groom Name: Henry M. Hill

Bride Name: Dell M. Fay
Wedding Date: Feb. 4, 1880
Clergy: F. A. Bisbee

~~~~~~~~~~~~~~~~~~

Page: 100-101
Groom Name: Seth D. Bradley
Bride Name: Abbie B. Drury
Wedding Date: Nov. 16, 1880
Clergy: F. A. Bisbee

~~~~~~~~~~~~~~~~~~

Page: 100-101
Groom Name: Chas. H. Spencer
Bride Name: Emiline Adams
Wedding Date: Feb. 16, 1881
Clergy: F. A. Bisbee

~~~~~~~~~~~~~~~~~~

Page: 102-103
Groom Name: Frank H. Barnard
Bride Name: Bessie A. Stevens
Wedding Date: April 21, 1881
Clergy: F. A. Bisbee

~~~~~~~~~~~~~~~~~~

Page: 102-103
Groom Name: John S. Ourish
Bride Name: Hulda M. Rich
Wedding Date: May 1881
Clergy: F. A. Bisbee

~~~~~~~~~~~~~~~~~~

Page: 102-103
Groom Name: Fred W. Cummings
Bride Name: Flora M. Wheeler

Wedding Date: June 11, 1881
Clergy: F. A. Bisbee

~~~~~~~~~~~~~~~~~~

Page: 102-103
Groom Name: Jos. C. Cotter
Bride Name: Ida Belcher
Wedding Date: Nov. 1881
Clergy: F. A. Bisbee
Variations in Book 2: Ada Belcher

~~~~~~~~~~~~~~~~~~

Page: 102-103
Groom Name: Ed. G. Desoe
Bride Name: Nettie Drury
Wedding Date: Dec. 5, 1881
Clergy: F. A. Bisbee

~~~~~~~~~~~~~~~~~~

Page: 102-103
Groom Name: Chas. M. Thompson
Bride Name: Lillie E. Brewer
Wedding Date: Dec. 8, 1881
Clergy: F. A. Bisbee

~~~~~~~~~~~~~~~~~~

Page: 102-103
Groom Name: Dennis Cunningham
Bride Name: Clara E. Belcher
Wedding Date: Jan. 25, 1882
Clergy: F. A. Bisbee

~~~~~~~~~~~~~~~~~~

Page: 102-103
Groom Name: James McRoberts
Bride Name: Martha J. McIntyre
Wedding Date: May 9, 1882
Clergy: F. A. Bisbee
Variations in Book 2: Martha J. McIntire

~~~~~~~~~~~~~~~~~~~

Page: 102-103
Groom Name: Fred C. Squires
Bride Name: Nellie Marsh
Wedding Date: July 6, 1882
Clergy: F. A. Bisbee
Variations in Book 2: July 8, 1882 [marriage date]

~~~~~~~~~~~~~~~~~~~

Page: 104-105
Groom Name: Wm. H. Parker
Bride Name: Mary B. Parmeter
Wedding Date: Sept. 23, 1882
Clergy: F. A. Bisbee

~~~~~~~~~~~~~~~~~~~

Page: 104-105
Groom Name: John E. Lamb
Bride Name: Clara A. Hammond
Wedding Date: Nov. 6, 1882
Clergy: F. A. Bisbee

~~~~~~~~~~~~~~~~~~~

Page: 104-105
Groom Name: Chas. H. Morgan
Bride Name: Mary D. Calhoun
Wedding Date: Oct. 19, 1882
Clergy: F. A. Bisbee

Page: 104-105
Groom Name: Frank M. Prouty
Bride Name: Mabel E. Kitredge
Wedding Date: Nov. 28, 1882
Clergy: F. A. Bisbee

~~~~~~~~~~~~~~~~~~~

Page: 104-105
Groom Name: Henry F. Copp
Bride Name: Lois B. Lamb
Wedding Date: Nov. 29
Clergy: F. A. Bisbee

~~~~~~~~~~~~~~~~~~~

Page: 104-105
Groom Name: Joseph C. Palamountain
Bride Name: Etta R. Slayton
Wedding Date: April 4, 1883
Clergy: F. A. Bisbee

~~~~~~~~~~~~~~~~~~~

Page: 104-105
Groom Name: [Blank] Bemis
Bride Name: Miss Addie Desoe
Wedding Date: Nov. 11, 1885
Clergy: J. M. Bartholomew

~~~~~~~~~~~~~~~~~~~

Page: 104-105
Groom Name: [Blank] Belcher
Bride Name: Miss [Blank]
Wedding Clergy: J. M. Bartholomew

~~~~~~~~~~~~~~~~~~~

Page: 104-105
Groom Name: Frank R. Heath
Bride Name: Clara M. Dennis
Wedding Date: June 22, 1887
Clergy: J. M. Bartholomew

~~~~~~~~~~~~~~~~~~

Page: 106-107
Groom Name: William H.
Hathaway
Bride Name: Cora E. Wilson
Wedding Date: June 30, 1887
Clergy: J. M. Bartholomew

~~~~~~~~~~~~~~~~~~

Page: 106-107
Groom Name: Henry H. Proctor
Bride Name: Edna Bemis
Wedding Date: Sept. 20, 1887
Clergy: J. M. Bartholomew

~~~~~~~~~~~~~~~~~~

Page: 106-107
Groom Name: Thomas J. Burkill
Bride Name: Minnie E. Draper
Wedding Date: Nov. 28, 1888
Clergy: J. S. Gledhill

~~~~~~~~~~~~~~~~~~

Page: 106-107
Groom Name: Louis H. Ingraham
Bride Name: Alice M. Stevenson
Wedding Date: May 29, 1889
Clergy: J. S. Gledhill

~~~~~~~~~~~~~~~~~~

Page: 106-107
Groom Name: Wm. E. Capen
Bride Name: Caroline Charters
Wedding Date: June 5, 1889
Clergy: J. S. Gledhill

~~~~~~~~~~~~~~~~~~

Page: 106-107
Groom Name: Geo. H. French
Bride Name: Gertrude L. Norton
Wedding Date: June 23, 1889
Clergy: J. S. Gledhill

~~~~~~~~~~~~~~~~~~

Page: 106-107
Groom Name: Chas. H. Collins
Bride Name: Mable A. Fay
Wedding Date: Sept. 11, 1889
Clergy: J. S. Gledhill

~~~~~~~~~~~~~~~~~~

Page: 106-107
Groom Name: Henry F. Corbin
Bride Name: Ella J. Watson
Wedding Date: Oct. 24, 1889
Clergy: J. S. Gledhill

~~~~~~~~~~~~~~~~~~

Page: 106-107
Groom Name: Martin L. Rodman
Bride Name: Mary E. Putnam
Wedding Date: Oct. 31, 1889
Clergy: J. S. Gledhill

~~~~~~~~~~~~~~~~~~

Page: 108-109
Groom Name: Thomas A. Forsythe
Bride Name: Ida E. Amidon
Wedding Date: Dec. 23, 1889
Clergy: J. S. Gledhill

~~~~~~~~~~~~~~~~~~~

Page: 108-109
Groom Name: John Prussia
Bride Name: Clara Morse
Wedding Date: April 20, 1890
Clergy: J. S. Gledhill

~~~~~~~~~~~~~~~~~~~

Page: 108-109
Groom Name: Elroy S. Hunter
Bride Name: Lydia M. Corlis
Wedding Date: June 14, 1890
Clergy: J. S. Gledhill

~~~~~~~~~~~~~~~~~~~

Page: 108-109
Groom Name: Geo. H. Woodbury
Bride Name: Minnie D. Fay
Wedding Date: July 12, 1890
Clergy: J. S. Gledhill

~~~~~~~~~~~~~~~~~~~

Page: 108-109
Groom Name: Chas. H. Adams
Bride Name: Jessie May Wise
Wedding Date: Oct. 20, 1890
Clergy: J. S. Gledhill

~~~~~~~~~~~~~~~~~~~

Page: 108-109
Groom Name: Edgar A. Abbott

Bride Name: Cora L. Prouty
Wedding Date: Feb. 4, 1891
Clergy: J. S. Gledhill

~~~~~~~~~~~~~~~~~~~

Page: 108-109
Groom Name: Alfonzo Cota
Bride Name: L. Edna Adams
Wedding Date: Feb. 28, 1891
Clergy: J. S. Gledhill

~~~~~~~~~~~~~~~~~~~

Page: 108-109
Groom Name: Herbert L. Houghton
Bride Name: Lottie E. Palmer
Wedding Date: April 7, 1891
Clergy: J. S. Gledhill

~~~~~~~~~~~~~~~~~~~

Page: 108-109
Groom Name: Henry H. Adams
Bride Name: Nellie Putnam
Wedding Date: April 15, 1891
Clergy: J. S. Gledhill

~~~~~~~~~~~~~~~~~~~

Page: 110-111
Groom Name: Henry P. Hambury
Bride Name: Gertrude L. Draper
Wedding Date: July 4, 1891
Clergy: J. S. Gledhill

~~~~~~~~~~~~~~~~~~~

Page: 110-111
Groom Name: Percy St. Clair
Bride Name: Annie E. Waltham

Wedding Date: July 25, 1891
Clergy: J. S. Gledhill

~~~~~~~~~~~~~~~~~~

Page: 110-111
Groom Name: Oscar Johnson
Bride Name: Emma Peterson
Wedding Date: Oct. 16, 1891
Clergy: J. S. Gledhill

~~~~~~~~~~~~~~~~~~

Page: 110-111
Groom Name: Napoleon Perry
Bride Name: Rosa Plante
Wedding Date: Feb. 27, 1893
Clergy: T. O. Marvin

~~~~~~~~~~~~~~~~~~

Page: 110-111
Groom Name: Frank X. Vincent
Bride Name: Emma Dupon
Wedding Date: May 12, 1893
Clergy: T. O. Marvin

~~~~~~~~~~~~~~~~~~

Page: 110-111
Groom Name: John Goodell Prouty
Occupation: Shoe Maker
Birth Place: Spencer
Father: Geo. Prouty
Mother: Mary Bemis
Bride Name: Ida Maud Howe
Birth Place: Spencer
Father: Ebenezer Howe
Wedding Date: Sept. 18, 1894
Clergy: T. O. Marvin

Page: 110-111
Groom Name: Frank Allen Hubbord, M. D.
Bride Name: Elizabeth Anna Wheeler
Birth Place: Spencer
Father: E. R. Wheeler, M. D.
Mother: Amelia Hamilton
Wedding Date: June 30, 1896
Clergy: C. W. Biddle

~~~~~~~~~~~~~~~~~~

Page: 110-111
Groom Name: Herbert H. Capen
Age: 42
Occupation: Merchant
Birth Place: Charlton
Father: Alfred
Mother: Mesia E. Sibley
Number of marriage: 2
Bride Name: Kate M. Prouty
Age: 35
Birth Place: Spencer
Father: Nathan H.
Mother: Cordia Holcomb
Number of marriage: 1
Wedding Place: Spencer, Mass.
Date: Jan. 17, 1899
Clergy: Edward C. Downey
Witness: Mrs. Grace Downey

~~~~~~~~~~~~~~~~~~

Page: 110-111
Groom Name: Everett E. Barns
Age: 39
Occupation: Shoe Operative
Birth Place: New Braintree
Father: Elbridge E.
Mother: Catherine Danahy
Number of marriage: 2

Bride Name: Rosa J. (Rooney) Griffin
Age: 28
Birth Place: Spencer
Father: James
Mother: Mary A. Bamson
Number of marriage: 2
Wedding Place: Spencer, Mass.
Date: Feb. 14, 1899
Clergy: Edward C. Downey
Witness: Mrs. G. S. Downey

~~~~~~~~~~~~~~~~~~

Page: 112-113
Groom Name: George H. Burkill
Age: 25
Occupation: Druggist
Birth Place: Hudson, Mass.
Father: James
Mother: Ellen M. Craith
Number of marriage: 1
Bride Name: Martha Jones
Age: 23
Birth Place: Spencer, Mass.
Father: Jarvis H.
Mother: Ella Bemis
Number of marriage: 1
Wedding Place: Bride's house, Spencer, Mass.
Date: June 27, 1899
Clergy: Edward C. Downey

~~~~~~~~~~~~~~~~~~

Page: 112-113
Groom Name: Linus H. Bacon
Age: 26
Occupation: Boot M'f'g
Birth Place: Spencer
Father: John E.
Mother: Mary J. Hersey

Number of marriage: 1
Bride Name: Edeith F. Howland
Age: 27
Birth Place: Oxford
Father: E. Harris
Mother: Mattie P. Carson
Number of marriage: 1
Wedding Place: Bride's house, Spencer, Mass.
Date: June 28, 1899
Clergy: Edward C. Downey
Witnesses: Will Bacon, Mr. Howland

~~~~~~~~~~~~~~~~~~

Page: 112-113
Groom Name: John W. Gale
Age: 38
Occupation: Farmer
Father: Chas. D.
Mother: H--rit G [or J] Moore
Number of marriage: 1
Bride Name: Alice M. Lyford
Age: 27
Birth Place: Spencer
Father: Joseph A.
Mother: Esther V. Howe
Number of marriage: 1
Wedding Place: Parsonage, Spencer, Mass.
Date: Oct. 11, 1899
Clergy: Edward C. Downey
Witnesses: Mrs. Downey

~~~~~~~~~~~~~~~~~~

Page: 112-113
Groom Name: Irwin Hazlehurst
Age: 21
Occupation: Boot Op.
Birth Place: Spencer

Father: Joseph
Mother: Ellen Anderson
Number of marriage: 1
Bride Name: Flora A. Richard
Age: 27
Birth Place: Spencer
Father: David T.
Mother: Anna Fenner
Number of marriage: 1
Wedding Place: Parsonage,
Spencer, Mass.
Date: Mar 24, 1900
Clergy: Edward C. Downey

~~~~~~~~~~~~~~~~~~

Page: 112-113
Groom Name: John W. Learned
Age: 57
Occupation: Merchant
Birth Place: Salem
Father: James M.
Mother: Mary Marble
Number of marriage: 2
Bride Name: Della Tripp
Weatherbee
Age: 63
Birth Place: RI
Father: Gilbert Tripp
Mother: Pheba Manchester
Number of marriage: 2
Wedding Place: Parsonage,
Spencer, Mass.
Date: June 20, 1900
Clergy: Edward C. Downey
Witnesses: Mr. Tripp, Mrs. Tripp

~~~~~~~~~~~~~~~~~~

Page: 112-113
Groom Name: Jonas Bemis, Jr.
Age: 27

Occupation: Farmer
Birth Place: Charlton
Father: Jonas
Mother: Harriet Hamilton
Number of marriage: 1
Bride Name: Minnie Florence
Adams
Age: 25
Birth Place: Brookfield
Father: Amasa
Mother: Olive Adams
Number of marriage: 1
Wedding Place: Parsonage,
Spencer, Mass.
Date: June 27, 1900
Clergy: Edward C. Downey
Witnesses: Mrs. Downey

~~~~~~~~~~~~~~~~~~

Page: 112-113
Groom Name: Charles J. Wilder
Age: 22
Occupation: Engineer
Birth Place: Brookfield
Father: William H.
Mother: Anistella Carr
Number of marriage: 1
Bride Name: Charlotte E. Bailey
Age: 21
Birth Place: Holliston
Father: Charles F.
Mother: Lora A. Allen
Number of marriage: 1
Wedding Place: Bride's house,
Spencer, Mass.
Date: July 15, 1900
Clergy: Edward C. Downey
Witnesses: W. H. Wilder, C. F.
Bailey

~~~~~~~~~~~~~~~~~~

Page: 112-113
Groom Name: John B. Carpenter
Age: 31
Occupation: Druggist
Birth Place: Brookfield
Father: Charles B.
Mother: Sarah L. Howaut [?]
Number of marriage: 1
Bride Name: Sarah B. Wilder
Age: 31
Occupation: Teacher
Birth Place: Brookfield
Father: William H.
Mother: Anistella A. Carr
Number of marriage: 1
Wedding Place: Univ. Church,
Spencer, Mass.
Date: Sept. 2, 1900
Clergy: Edward C. Downey

~~~~~~~~~~~~~~~~~

Page: 112-113
Groom Name: Willard David
Ross
Age: 23
Occupation: Boot op.
Birth Place: Hardwick
Father: Samuel
Mother: Jessie Kennedy
Number of marriage: 1
Bride Name: Minnie Grace Howe
Age: 30
Occupation: At Home
Birth Place: Spencer
Father: Ebenezer
Mother: Mary A. Hobbs
Number of marriage: 1
Wedding Place: Bride 's House,
Spencer
Date: May 29, 1902
Clergy: Frank L. Masseck

Page: 114-115
Groom Name: George D. Muzzy
Age: 28
Occupation: Salesman
Birth Place: Spencer
Father: Charles Muzzy, 2d
Mother: Berrie M. Cummings
Number of marriage: 1
Bride Name: Fanny Laura Bacon
Age: 25
Occupation: At home
Birth Place: Spencer
Father: Arthur B. Bacon
Mother: Ella Farmer Kent
Number of marriage: 1
Wedding Place: Spencer
Date: Sept. 16, 1902
Clergy: Frank L. Masseck

~~~~~~~~~~~~~~~~~

Page: 114-115
Groom Name: Batise Carter
Age: 40
Occupation: Farm laborer
Birth Place: Roxton Pond,
Canada
Father: A. Carter
Mother: E. Duferner
Number of marriage: 2
Bride Name: Olive Rossier
Age: 22
Occupation: Housekeeper
Birth Place: Montgomery, Vt.
Father: Samuel Rossier
Mother: Betsy Parry
Number of marriage: 1
Wedding Place: Spencer
Date: Aug. 18, 1902
Clergy: Frank L. Masseck

~~~~~~~~~~~~~~~~~

Page: 114-115
Groom Name: Arthur Perry Wilson
Age: 20—Parents' consent filed
Occupation: Farmer
Birth Place: Spencer
Father: Oscar W. Wilson
Mother: Lydia A. Bemis
Number of marriage: 1
Bride Name: Maud Ethel Hoyle
Age: 15—Permission granted by Probate Court
Occupation: At Home
Birth Place: Worcester
Father: Fred Loring Hoyle
Mother: Alma Bertha Jenison
Number of marriage: 1
Wedding Place: Spencer
Date: January 26, 1903
Clergy: Frank L. Masseck

~~~~~~~~~~~~~~~~~~

Page: 114-115
Groom Name: Joseph Henry Saunders
Age: 30
Occupation: Physician
Birth Place: Haverhill
Father: Oliver Hubbard Saunders
Mother: Elizabeth McKay
Number of marriage: 1
Bride Name: Carrie Hunter Sibley
Age: 27
Occupation: At Home
Birth Place: Spencer
Father: Emory Francis Sibley
Mother: May Paris Bullard
Number of marriage: 1
Wedding Place: Spencer
Date: April 22, 1903

Clergy: Frank L. Masseck

~~~~~~~~~~~~~~~~~~

Page: 114-115
Groom Name: Philip Hildreth Robinson
Age: 24
Occupation: Hardware Dealer
Birth Place: Newton
Father: John Howard Robinson
Mother: Helen Frances Barnes
Number of marriage: 1
Bride Name: Nina Gertrude Eaton
Age: 25
Occupation: At Home
Birth Place: No. Brookfield
Father: Frank S. Eaton
Mother: Alice J. Hill
Number of marriage: 1
Wedding Place: No. Brookfield
Date: June 16, 1903
Clergy: Frank L. Masseck

~~~~~~~~~~~~~~~~~~

Page: 114-115
Groom Name: Arthur A. Sandland
Age: 20
Occupation: Jeweler
Birth Place: North Attleborough
Father: Alvin T. Sandland
Mother: Adela E. Ryan
Number of marriage: 1
Bride Name: Amelia R. Allen
Age: 17—Parents' consent filed with Town Clerk
Occupation: Jeweler
Birth Place: North Attleborough
Father: Abner C. Allen

Mother: Mary A. Collins
Number of marriage: 1
Wedding Place: North
Attleborough
Date: July 23, 1903
Clergy: Frank L. Masseck

~~~~~~~~~~~~~~~~~~

Page: 114-115
Groom Name: Leslie E. Mann
Age: 27
Occupation: Mechanic
Birth Place: Milford
Father: Henry M.
Mother: Ella F. Kendall
Number of marriage: 1
Bride Name: Nora E. Sisson
Age: 20
Occupation: None
Birth Place: Stonington, Conn.
Father: Frank
Mother: Nellie Mullein
Number of marriage: 1
Wedding Place: Spencer
Date: August 12, 1903
Clergy: Frank L. Masseck

~~~~~~~~~~~~~~~~~~

Page: 114-115
Groom Name: Forrest L. Mitchell
Age: 38
Occupation: Insurance
Birth Place: Pownal, Me.
Father: Albert L.
Mother: Elvira Seabury
Number of marriage: 1
Bride Name: Minnie A. Moore
Age: 32
Occupation: Milliner
Birth Place: No. Whitefield, Me.

Father: William A.
Mother: Lastima Collison
Number of marriage: 1
Wedding Place: Spencer
Date: August 19, 1903
Clergy: Frank L. Masseck

~~~~~~~~~~~~~~~~~~

Page: 114-115
Groom Name: Napoleon
Papineau
Age: 38
Occupation: Decorator & Paper-
hanger
Birth Place: Attleboro
Father: Joseph
Mother: Emily Pearl
Number of marriage: 2
Bride Name: Mary Burns
Age: 33
Occupation: Boot op.
Birth Place: Spencer
Father: Robert
Mother: Mary Ann
Number of marriage: 1
Wedding Place: Spencer
Date: August 23, 1903
Clergy: Frank L. Masseck
Witnesses: Divorced, Decree Nisi
granted July 15, 1903

~~~~~~~~~~~~~~~~~~

Page: 116-117
Groom Name: Harry G. Nichols
Age: 22
Occupation: Boot op.
Birth Place: Worcester
Father: George H.
Mother: Martha A. Lamb
Number of marriage: 1

Bride Name: Harriet E. Woodbury
Age: 21
Occupation: At home
Birth Place: Spencer
Father: William W.
Mother: Ellen M. Garfield
Number of marriage: 1
Wedding Place: Spencer
Date: Sept. 3, 1903
Clergy: Frank L. Masseck

~~~~~~~~~~~~~~~~~~

Page: 116-117
Groom Name: Frank T. Prouty
Age: 54
Occupation: Boot op.
Birth Place: Worcester
Father: Joseph
Mother: Clair Tatman
Number of marriage: 2
Bride Name: Mary E. Sargent
Age: 44
Occupation: Housekeeper
Birth Place: N. Brookfield
Father: Solomon Brigham
Mother: Martha A. Kendrick
Number of marriage: 1
Wedding Place: Spencer
Date: Nov. 3, 1903
Clergy: Frank L. Masseck

~~~~~~~~~~~~~~~~~~

Page: 116-117
Groom Name: Walter Edward Sibley
Age: 25
Occupation: Farmer

Birth Place: Spencer
Father: Freeman
Mother: Amanda Dean
Number of marriage: 1
Bride Name: Alice May Wilson
Age: 18
Occupation: At home
Birth Place: Spencer
Father: Oscar W.
Mother: Lydia A. Bemis
Number of marriage: 1
Wedding Place: Spencer
Date: Nov. 10, 1903
Clergy: Frank L. Masseck

~~~~~~~~~~~~~~~~~~

Page: 116-117
Groom Name: Fred Howard Crockett
Age: 27
Occupation: Book-keeper
Birth Place: Exeter, N.H.
Father: Frank S.
Mother: Martha A. Merrill
Number of marriage: 1
Bride Name: Mary Eleanor Bryant
Age: 31
Occupation: Clerk
Birth Place: Springfield
Father: Wellington S.
Mother: Lillian M. Spear
Number of marriage: 1
Wedding Place: Spencer
Date: Dec. 7, 1903
Clergy: Frank L. Masseck

~~~~~~~~~~~~~~~~~~

Page: 116-117
Groom Name: Israel Joseph Hinckley
Age: 46
Occupation: Carriage Painter
Birth Place: Spencer
Father: Peter
Mother: Pauline E. Brooks
Number of marriage: 1
Bride Name: Mary Lydia (Corliss) Hunter
Age: 34
Occupation: At home
Birth Place: Sutton, Vt.
Father: Dennison
Mother: Christania Orcott
Number of marriage: 2
Wedding Place: Spencer
Date: Dec. 16, 1903
Clergy: Frank L. Masseck

~~~~~~~~~~~~~~~~~~

Page: 116-117
Groom Name: Lawrence W. Putnam
Age: 25
Occupation: Boot up.
Birth Place: Spencer
Father: Archelaus D.
Mother: Jennie P. Lackey
Number of marriage: 1
Bride Name: Edith H. Bellows
Age: 21
Occupation: At home
Birth Place: Spencer
Father: Arthur L.
Mother: Eva Lenox
Number of marriage: 1
Wedding Place: Spencer
Date: June 5, 1904
Clergy: Frank L. Masseck

Page: 116-117
Groom Name: William W. Taylor
Age: 27
Occupation: Carpenter
Birth Place: Springfield
Father: Charles G.
Mother: Emma S. Spencer
Number of marriage: 1
Bride Name: Cora E. Leonard
Age: 36
Occupation: Dancing teacher
Birth Place: Spencer
Father: Abraham P.
Mother: Lucy M. Spencer
Number of marriage: 1
Wedding Place: Spencer
Date: Sept. 4, 1904
Clergy: Frank L. Masseck

~~~~~~~~~~~~~~~~~~

Page: 116-117
Groom Name: Henry H. Hunt
Age: 25
Occupation: Farmer
Birth Place: Enfield
Father: Daniel
Mother: Eliza Hewitt
Number of marriage: 1
Bride Name: Ellen Louise Jenkins
Age: 24
Occupation: At home
Birth Place: Whitinsville
Father: Charles T.
Mother: Amy M. Brown
Number of marriage: 1
Wedding Place: Spencer
Date: April 3, 1915
Clergy: Frank L. Masseck

~~~~~~~~~~~~~~~~~~

Page: 116-117
Groom Name: Wm. W. Austin
Age: 26
Occupation: Electrician
Birth Place: Salem, Mass.
Number of marriage: 1
Bride Name: Edna H. Johnson
Age: 26
Occupation: Teacher
Birth Place: Spencer, Mass.
Father: Alfred H.
Mother: Anna Bullard
Number of marriage: 1
Wedding Place: Spencer, at the residence of Dexter Bullard
Date: Sept. 15, 1906
Clergy: Asa M. Bradley
Witnesses: Dexter Bullard, Dr. Morse, Phebe Johnson

~~~~~~~~~~~~~~~~~~

Page: 118-119
Groom Name: Harry L. Auger
Age: 20—Consent of Charles A. Auger filed to the marriage of the Groom.
Occupation: Hostler
Birth Place: Worcester
Father: Charles A.
Mother: Bertha Huber
Number of marriage: 1
Bride Name: Geneva Farmer
Age: 18
Occupation: Shoe operative
Birth Place: Spencer
Father: Harry
Mother: Julia E. McKernan
Number of marriage: 1
Wedding Place: Spencer
Date: Sept. 29, 1906
Clergy: Asa M. Bradley

Witnesses: Hannah C. Emery, Mary E. Bradley

~~~~~~~~~~~~~~~~~~

Page: 118-119
Groom Name: Chester C. Lovell
Age: 24
Occupation: Clerk
Birth Place: Spencer
Father: Ethan H. Lovell
Mother: Anne Cross
Number of marriage: 1
Bride Name: Marion J. Jones
Age: 22
Occupation: Bookkeeper
Birth Place: Spencer
Father: Jarvis H. Jones
Mother: Ellen M. Bemis
Number of marriage: 1
Wedding Place: Spencer
Date: Oct. 2, 1906
Clergy: Asa M. Bradley
Witnesses: Josephine Lovell, [blank] Prentis

~~~~~~~~~~~~~~~~~~

Page: 118-119
Groom Name: William J. Murray
Age: 38
Occupation: Moulder
Birth Place: Mass.
Father: Francis Murray
Mother: Margaret McGowan
Number of marriage: 1
Bride Name: Rose Rivers (Knowles)
Age: 24
Occupation: Stenographer
Birth Place: Webster, Mass.
Father: Peter Rivers

Mother: Emma
Number of marriage: 2 (D)
Wedding Place: Spencer
Date: Jan. 8, 1907
Clergy: Asa M. Bradley
Witnesses: Brother of Bride and his wife, Mrs. A. M. Bradley

~~~~~~~~~~~~~~~~~~

Page: 118-119
Groom Name: Arthur W. Hamilton
Age: 21
Occupation: Gardener
Birth Place: N. B.
Father: William F. Hamilton
Mother: Henrietta Higgins
Number of marriage: 1
Bride Name: Julia E. McKernin Fenner
Age: 33
Occupation: Domestic
Birth Place: N. B.
Father: Charles McKernin
Mother: Catherine McDonnell
Number of marriage: 2d (w)
Wedding Place: Spencer
Date: June 26, 1907
Clergy: Asa M. Bradley
Witnesses: Henry F. Auger, Mrs. Henry F. Auger

~~~~~~~~~~~~~~~~~~

Page: 118-119
Groom Name: Geo. E. Trull
Age: 55
Occupation: Shoemaker
Birth Place: Andover, Mass.
Father: John Trull
Mother: Mary B. Brown

Number of marriage: 2 (w)
Bride Name: Theresina Peabody
Age: 53
Occupation: Operative
Birth Place: Nova Scotia
Father: Bradford B. Freeman
Mother: Elizabeth Morine
Number of marriage: 2 (w)
Wedding Place: Spencer - Ceremony at the residence of F. A. Barr. Bride sister to Mrs. Barr. Both fathers residents of Lynn, Mass.
Date: Oct. 12, 1907
Clergy: Asa M. Bradley
Witnesses: F. A. Barr, Mrs F. A. Barr

~~~~~~~~~~~~~~~~~~

Page: 118-119
Groom Name: Alton F. Prouty
Age: 25
Occupation: Clerk
Birth Place: Spencer
Father: Frank T. Prouty
Mother: Emma Brewer
Number of marriage: 1
Bride Name: Antine A. Goodnow
Age: 22
Occupation: Teacher
Birth Place: Spencer
Father: Geo. A. Goodnow
Mother: Jennie M. Clark
Number of marriage: 1
Wedding Place: Spencer - Ceremony at the residence of Geo. A. Goodnow at 2 p.m.
Date: Dec. 18, 1907
Clergy: Asa M. Bradley
Witnesses: Josephine Goodnow, Ralph Prouty

Page: 118-119
Groom Name: Ward J. Furbush
Age: 42
Occupation: Carriage painter
Birth Place: New Vineyard, Me.
Father: Ward Furbush
Mother: Hannah Trask
Number of marriage: 2
Bride Name: Addie Clark
Age: 44
Occupation: Shoe operative
Birth Place: Brattleboro, Vt.
Father: Joseph Papineau
Mother: un
Number of marriage: 2
Wedding Place: Spencer
Date: April 9th 1908
Clergy: Asa M. Bradley
Witnesses: a son of Groom and Wife of Bride's Son

~~~~~~~~~~~~~~~~~~

Page: 118-119
Groom Name: Foster Reed Wheeler
Age: 25
Occupation: Customs Broker
Birth Place: Spencer
Father: Edward R. Wheeler
Mother: Amelia R. Rhoeder
Number of marriage: 1
Bride Name: Eleanor May Davis
Age: 23
Occupation: At home
Birth Place: Spencer
Father: Geo. F. Davis
Mother: Eleanor J. Amidon
Wedding Place: Somerville, Spencer [? both are listed]—Ceremony at the residence of Geo. F. Davis

Date: April 30th 1908
Clergy: Asa M. Bradley
Witnesses: Miss Mitchell, Mr. Ham

~~~~~~~~~~~~~~~~~~

Page: 118-119
Groom Name: Geo. R. Winslow
Age: 29
Occupation: Shoe operative
Birth Place: Whitman, Mass.
Father: Thos. E. Winslow
Mother: Florence A. Reed
Number of marriage: 1
Bride Name: Lucy J. Pepper
Age: 38
Occupation: Shoe operative
Birth Place: Hardwick
Father: Ashbel Pepper
Mother: Martha Silsby
Number of marriage: 1
Wedding Place: Spencer
Date: July 4th 1908
Clergy: Asa M. Bradley
Witnesses: Gertrude Kimball, Mrs. Bradley

~~~~~~~~~~~~~~~~~~

Page: 120-121
Groom Name: Robert C. Dwelly
Age: 22
Occupation: Farmer
Birth Place: Oakham
Father: Edwin H. Dwelly
Mother: Emma F. Robinson
Number of marriage: 1
Bride Name: Fannie E. Proctor
Age: 20
Occupation: Office Clerk
Birth Place: Spencer

Father: Henry Proctor
Mother: Edna F. Bemis
Number of marriage: 1
Wedding Place: Spencer
Date: May 29, 1909
Clergy: Asa M. Bradley
Witnesses: Mrs. Bradley, Mrs. Emery

~~~~~~~~~~~~~~~~~~~

Page: 120-121
Groom Name: George A. Putney
Age: 26
Occupation: Merchant
Birth Place: Charlton
Father: Albert A. Putney
Mother: Frances Newcomb
Number of marriage: 1
Bride Name: Elsie M. Stratton
Age: 20
Occupation: At Home
Birth Place: Brookfield
Father: Richard V. Stratton
Mother: Mary D. Pierce
Number of marriage: 1
Wedding Place: East Brookfield—Ceremony at the home of the Bride's parents in East Brookfield
Date: Sept. 8, 1909
Clergy: Asa M. Bradley
Witnesses: R. V. Stratton, Mrs. R. V. Stratton

~~~~~~~~~~~~~~~~~~

Page: 120-121
Groom Name: Arthur E. Murdock
Occupation: Insurance Agent
Birth Place: Spencer

Father: Edward A. Murdock
Number of marriage: 1
Bride Name: Phebe Chandler Johnson
Occupation: Teacher
Birth Place: Spencer
Father: Alfred H. Johnson
Mother: Annie Bullard
Number of marriage: 1
Wedding Place: Spencer— Ceremony at the home of the Bride.
Date: Oct. 3, 1910
Clergy: Rev. Geo. L. Perin, D. D.

~~~~~~~~~~~~~~~~~~~~~~

DEATH NOTES

~~~~~~~~~~~~~~~~~~~~~~

Information on the deaths of members of the Universalist Church are located in Book 1, page 150-161. There are six columns with the following headings: no.; name; date; age; date of burial; and remarks and references. Finally, we will include the additional information found only in Book 2. Not every column is filled in for each person.

In some instances, a date is given only in the "date" column and not in the "date of burial" column. It is unclear whether the given date refers to death or burial.

Dates were transcribed as they appeared in the original.

58

Standardized punctuation was used. [ ] indicates words added by the editor. [ ] around data indicates a best guess as to what was written.

In column 1 in Book 1, the name of the officiating clergy is listed; that information will be listed under "pastor." Page number and line number are listed here for convenience.

~~~~~~~~~~~~~~~~~~~~~
DEATHS
~~~~~~~~~~~~~~~~~~~~~

Page: 150   [Line]: [1]
Name: Mrs. Abbie Parthenia Hill
Date: Nov. 15, 1907
Age: 64-4-11
Date of Burial: Nov. 18
Remarks: At North Brookfield at the home of F. N. Eaton
Pastor: Rev. A. M. Bradley

~~~~~~~~~~~~~~~~~~

Page: 150   [Line]: [2]
Name: Eleta Darling
Date: Dec. 29, 1907
Age: 40
Date of Burial: Dec. 31
Remarks: Grave service at Pine Grove. Died in Boston. Niece of Mrs. Warren Livermore.
Pastor: Rev. A. M. Bradley

~~~~~~~~~~~~~~~~~~

Page: 150   [Line]: [3]
Name: Mrs. Amelia R. Wheeler

Date: Jan. 21, 1908
Age: 67-6-5
Date of Burial: Jan. 23
Remarks: Widow of Dr. E. R. Wheeler. Died at Taunton, Mass.
Pastor: Rev. A. M. Bradley

~~~~~~~~~~~~~~~~~~~~

Page: 150   [Line]: [4]
Name: Mrs. Laura A. Stone
Date: Feb. 11, 1908
Age: 69-6-12
Date of Burial: Feb. 14
Remarks: Wife of Henry R. Stone of Sturbridge Four Corners.
Pastor: Rev. A. M. Bradley

~~~~~~~~~~~~~~~~~~

Page: 150   [Line]: [5]
Name: James R. Black
Date: Feb. 15, 1908
Age: 70-3-15
Date of Burial: Feb. 16
Remarks: An old soldier. Farmed for Kingsley's. Husband of Caroline B. Black, p. 160
Pastor: Rev. A. M. Bradley

~~~~~~~~~~~~~~~~~~~~

Page: 150   [Line]: [6]
Name: Maria Sherwin Adams
Date: Feb. 20, 1908
Age: 88-3
Date of Burial: Feb. 22
Remarks: Mother of Mrs. Paul Sibley
Pastor: Rev. A. M. Bradley

Page: 150   [Line]: [7]
Name: Mrs. Jerusha Ann Boyden
Date: Feb. 25, 1908
Age: 84-1-3
Date of Burial: Feb. 29
Remarks: Wife of John Boyden, page 156
Pastor: Rev. A. M. Bradley

~~~~~~~~~~~~~~~~~~

Page: 150   [Line]: [8]
Name: Frank H. Thompson
Date of Burial: April 13
Remarks: Died Brockton. Buried North Brookfield
Pastor: Rev. A. M. Bradley

~~~~~~~~~~~~~~~~~~

Page: 150   [Line]: [9]
Name: Mrs. Adeline Drury
Date: April 13, 1908
Age: 75-3-9
Date of Burial: April 16
Remarks: Wife of Chandler Drury, p. 157
Pastor: Rev. A. M. Bradley

~~~~~~~~~~~~~~~~~~

Page: 150   [Line]: [10]
Name: Harold H. Carpenter
Date: Jan. 6, 1907
Age: 25
Date of Burial: April 18, 1908
Remarks: A soldier in U.S. Army. Died in Cuba of typhoid fever. Buried Brookfield.
Pastor: Rev. A. M. Bradley

~~~~~~~~~~~~~~~~~~

Page: 150   [Line]: [11]
Name: John Gallup Wood
Date: May 26, 1908
Age: 71-4-20
Date of Burial: May 28
Remarks: At East Brookfield
Pastor: Rev. A. M. Bradley

~~~~~~~~~~~~~~~~~~

Page: 150   [Line]: [12]
Name: Sarah Howes Prouty
Date: Oct. 1, 1907 [This record out of proper order.]
Age: 46-2-11
Date of Burial: Oct. 4, 1907
Remarks: Member of Church; a Trustee of Parish
Pastor: Rev. A. M. Bradley

~~~~~~~~~~~~~~~~~~

Page: 150   [Line]: [13]
Name: William P. Cowee
Date: July 6, 1908
Age: 82-9-13
Date of Burial: July 9, 1908
Remarks: At Warren. Brother to Mrs. A. J. Canfield and Mrs. D. I. Darting [?]
Pastor: Rev. A. M. Bradley

~~~~~~~~~~~~~~~~~~

Page: 150   [Line]: [14]
Name: Rosella A. Barton
Date: Aug. 28, 1908
Age: 31, less 5 days
Date of Burial: Aug. 30, 1908
Remarks: D. of Mrs. Lottie Barton, p. 156; Member of Church.

Pastor: Rev. A. M. Bradley

~~~~~~~~~~~~~~~~~~~

Page: 150   [Line]: [15]
Name: Sarah Jane Howland
Date: Sept. 21, 1908
Age: 60-5-5
Date of Burial: Sept. 24, 1908
Remarks: A prominent worker in Social life of Ch.
Pastor: Rev. A. M. Bradley

~~~~~~~~~~~~~~~~~~~

Page: 150   [Line]: [16]
Name: Mrs. Susan E. Eaton
Date: Nov. 10, 1908
Age: 76-2-10
Date of Burial: Nov. 12
Remarks: Wife of H. R. Eaton, North Brookfield
Pastor: Rev. A. M. Bradley

~~~~~~~~~~~~~~~~~~~

Page: 150   [Line]: [17]
Name: Daniel W. Adams
Date: Jan. 11, 1909
Age: 75-2-21
Date of Burial: Jan. 14
Remarks: Husband of Harriet E. Adams
Pastor: Rev. A. M. Bradley

~~~~~~~~~~~~~~~~~~~

Page: 150   [Line]: [18]
Name: Mrs. Addie M. Hamilton
Date: April 7, 1909
Age: 65-10-3
Date of Burial: Apr. 9

Remarks: Wife of Benj. F. Hamilton
Pastor: Rev. A. M. Bradley

~~~~~~~~~~~~~~~~~~~

Page: 150   [Line]: [19]
Name: Mrs. Phebe Barr
Date: April 14, 1909
Date of Burial: April 17
Remarks: Wife of Matt Barr of New York
Pastor: Rev. A. M. Bradley

~~~~~~~~~~~~~~~~~~~

Page: 150   [Line]: [20]
Name: Mrs. Mary W. Moore
Date: May 24, 1909
Age: 74-1-17
Date of Burial: May 26
Pastor: Rev. A. M. Bradley

~~~~~~~~~~~~~~~~~~~

Page: 150   [Line]: [21]
Name: Marshall D. Barr
Date: May 29, 1909
Date of Burial: June 3
Remarks: Son of E. G. Barr. Died Sandusky, Ohio
Pastor: Rev. A. M. Bradley

~~~~~~~~~~~~~~~~~~~

Page: 150   [Line]: [22]
Name: Fred A. Hamilton
Date: June 4, 1909
Age: 39-7-10
Date of Burial: June 7
Remarks: Son of Benj. F. and Addie Hamilton; alcoholism; d.

Boston. Fall cutting artery and d. of hemorage
Pastor: Rev. A. M. Bradley

~~~~~~~~~~~~~~~~~~

Page: 150   [Line]: [23]
Name: Mrs. Maria P. Proctor
Date: July 27, 1909
Age: 68-1-27
Date of Burial: July 29
Remarks: Wife of Josiah Proctor
Pastor: Rev. A. M. Bradley

~~~~~~~~~~~~~~~~~~

Page: 150   [Line]: [24]
Name: Mrs. Sarah Eldredge Capen
Date of Burial: July 29
Remarks: Died at Rockford, Ills.
Pastor: Rev. A. M. Bradley

~~~~~~~~~~~~~~~~~~

Page: 150   [Line]: [25]
Name: Infant child of Albert Sauveur
Date of Burial: Aug. 6
Remarks: Died in Paris, and laid some months in receiving vault.
Pastor: Rev. A. M. Bradley

~~~~~~~~~~~~~~~~~~

Page: 150   [Line]: [26]
Name: Mrs. Josephine Desoe
Date: Aug. 24, 1909
Age: 73
Date of Burial: Aug. 27
Remarks: Wife of Joseph Desoe,

p 154; Buried at Hope Cem., Worcester
Pastor: Rev. A. M. Bradley

~~~~~~~~~~~~~~~~~~

Page: 150   [Line]: [27]
Name: Warren J. Livermore
Date: Sept 9, 1909
Age: 74-8-4
Date of Burial: Sept. 13
Remarks: Funeral on the afternoon of Sept. 12th. Died at East Wareham, Mass.
Pastor: Rev. A. M. Bradley

~~~~~~~~~~~~~~~~~~

Page: 151   [Line]: [1]
Name: Mrs. Mary Lois Barr
Date: Sept. 14, 1909
Age: 35-11-5
Date of Burial: Sept. 16
Remarks: 2d wife of Alton H. Barr
Pastor: Rev. A. M. Bradley

~~~~~~~~~~~~~~~~~~

Page: 151   [Line]: [2]
Name: Ephraim G. Barr
Date: Dec. 1, 1909
Age: 82-1-23
Date of Burial: Dec. 5
Pastor: Rev. A. M. Bradley

~~~~~~~~~~~~~~~~~~

Page: 151   [Line]: [3]
Name: Mrs. Fannie Dwelly
Date: April 26, 1912
Age: 23-8

Date of Burial: April 28
Remarks: wife of Robert Dwelly;
daughter of Henry & Edna
(Bemis) Proctor
Pastor: G. F. Babbitt

~~~~~~~~~~~~~~~~~~

Page: 152   [Line]: [1]
Name: Lucia May Sumner
Date: Oct. 3, 1877
Pastor: Rev. F. A. Bisbee

~~~~~~~~~~~~~~~~~~

Page: 152   [Line]: [2]
Name: Mrs. Howe
Date: Dec. 22, 1877
Pastor: Rev. F. A. Bisbee
~~~~~~~~~~~~~~~~~~

Page: 152   [Line]: [3]
Name: Mr. Slayton
Pastor: Rev. F. A. Bisbee

~~~~~~~~~~~~~~~~~~

Page: 152   [Line]: [4]
Name: Mrs. Barr
Date: 1878
Pastor: Rev. F. A. Bisbee

~~~~~~~~~~~~~~~~~~

Page: 152   [Line]: [5]
Name: Mrs. Harris Howland
Pastor: Rev. F. A. Bisbee

~~~~~~~~~~~~~~~~~~

Page: 152   [Line]: [6]
Name: Baby twins of W. A. Sloane

Date: Aug 1879
Pastor: Rev. F. A. Bisbee

~~~~~~~~~~~~~~~~~~

Page: 152   [Line]: [7]
Name: Mr. Lyford
Pastor: Rev. F. A. Bisbee

~~~~~~~~~~~~~~~~~~

Page: 152   [Line]: [8]
Name: Mr. Adams
Date: Nov. 14, 1879
Remarks: Brookfield
Pastor: Rev. F. A. Bisbee

~~~~~~~~~~~~~~~~~~

Page: 152   [Line]: [9]
Name: Louise Cole
Date: Jan. 13, 1880
Pastor: Rev. F. A. Bisbee
~~~~~~~~~~~~~~~~~~

Page: 152   [Line]: [10]
Name: Mrs. Day
Date: Feb. 9, 1880
Remarks: Oakham
Pastor: Rev. F. A. Bisbee

~~~~~~~~~~~~~~~~~~

Page: 152   [Line]: [11]
Name: Chas. Bemis
Date: Feb. 10, 1880
Pastor: Rev. F. A. Bisbee

~~~~~~~~~~~~~~~~~~

Page: 152   [Line]: [12]
Name: Mr. Dustin

Date: Nov. 14, 1880
Pastor: Rev. F. A. Bisbee

~~~~~~~~~~~~~~~~~~

Page: 152   [Line]: [13]
Name: Mr. E. M. Cole
Date: 1880
Pastor: Rev. F. A. Bisbee

~~~~~~~~~~~~~~~~~~

Page: 152   [Line]: [14]
Name: Mr. Adams
Pastor: Rev. F. A. Bisbee
Additions from Book 2:
Brookfield

~~~~~~~~~~~~~~~~~~

Page: 81   [Line]: []
Name: child at Spencer Depot
Pastor: Rev. F. A. Bisbee
Additions from Book 2:
Grandchild of Frank Drury.
Found only in Book 2.

~~~~~~~~~~~~~~~~~~

Page: 152   [Line]: [15]
Name: Mrs. Howe
Pastor: Rev. F. A. Bisbee

~~~~~~~~~~~~~~~~~~

Page: 152   [Line]: [16]
Name: Mr. White
Remarks: Brookfield
Pastor: Rev. F. A. Bisbee
Additions from Book 2: Jan. 13,
1881

Page: 152   [Line]: [17]
Name: Brayman Bemis
Date: Jan. 27, 1881
Pastor: Rev. F. A. Bisbee
Additions from Book 2: Jan. 13,
1881

~~~~~~~~~~~~~~~~~~

Page: 152   [Line]: [18]
Name: Daniel Gibbs
Date: Feb. 11, 1881
Pastor: Rev. F. A. Bisbee
Additions from Book 2: Jan. 13,
1881

~~~~~~~~~~~~~~~~~~

Page: 152   [Line]: [19]
Name: Baby of Dr. Wheeler
Date: Apr. 1, 1881
Pastor: Rev. F. A. Bisbee
Additions from Book 2: Jan. 13,
1881

~~~~~~~~~~~~~~~~~~

Page: 152   [Line]: [20]
Name: Mr. Capen
Date: May 1881
Remarks: Brookfield
Pastor: Rev. F. A. Bisbee
Additions from Book 2: Jan. 13,
1881

~~~~~~~~~~~~~~~~~~

Page: 152   [Line]: [21]
Name: John Bemis
Date: July 1, 1881
Pastor: Rev. F. A. Bisbee

Additions from Book 2: Jan. 13, 1881

~~~~~~~~~~~~~~~~~~

Page: 152   [Line]: [22]
Name: Baby of Mr. Bemis
Date: Aug. 20, 1881
Pastor: Rev. F. A. Bisbee
Additions from Book 2: Jan. 13, 1881

~~~~~~~~~~~~~~~~~~

Page: 152   [Line]: [23]
Name: Baby of Chas. Sibley
Date: Aug. 22, 1881
Pastor: Rev. F. A. Bisbee
Additions from Book 2: Jan. 13, 1881

~~~~~~~~~~~~~~~~~~

Page: 152   [Line]: [24]
Name: Mr. Adams
Date: Sept. 1881
Remarks: Brookfield
Pastor: Rev. F. A. Bisbee
Additions from Book 2: Jan. 13, 1881

~~~~~~~~~~~~~~~~~~

Page: 152   [Line]: [25]
Name: [blank] Skinner
Date: Oct. 1881
Remarks: Palmer, Mass.
Pastor: Rev. F. A. Bisbee
Additions from Book 2: Jan. 13, 1881

~~~~~~~~~~~~~~~~~~

Page: 152   [Line]: [26]
Name: Clara Stockwell
Date: Feb. 2, 1882
Pastor: Rev. F. A. Bisbee
Additions from Book 2: Jan. 13, 1881

~~~~~~~~~~~~~~~~~~

Page: 152   [Line]: [27]
Name: Mrs. Barr
Date: Feb. 12, 1882
Pastor: Rev. F. A. Bisbee
Additions from Book 2: Jan. 13, 1881

~~~~~~~~~~~~~~~~~~

Page: 154   [Line]: [1]
Name: Mr. Worthington
Date: Feb. 15, 1882
Pastor: Rev F. A. Bisbee
Additions from Book 2: Jan. 13, 1881

~~~~~~~~~~~~~~~~~~

Page: 154   [Line]: [2]
Name: Mrs. Hammond
Date: Mch. 20, 1882
Pastor: Rev F. A. Bisbee
Additions from Book 2: Jan. 13, 1881

~~~~~~~~~~~~~~~~~~

Page: 154   [Line]: [3]
Name: Mrs. Ball
Date: June 3, 1881
Pastor: Rev F. A. Bisbee
Additions from Book 2: Jan. 13, 1881

Page: 154   [Line]: [4]
Name: Mr. Foster
Date: July 18, 1882
Pastor: Rev F. A. Bisbee
Additions from Book 2: Jan. 13, 1881

~ ~ ~ ~ ~ ~ ~ ~ ~ ~ ~ ~ ~ ~ ~ ~ ~ ~

Page: 154   [Line]: [5]
Name: Mr. Mason
Date: Aug. 5, 1882
Remarks: Cortland, N. Y.
Pastor: Rev F. A. Bisbee
Additions from Book 2: Jan. 13, 1881

~ ~ ~ ~ ~ ~ ~ ~ ~ ~ ~ ~ ~ ~ ~ ~ ~ ~

Page: 154   [Line]: [6]
Name: Mr. Moulton
Date: Oct. 9, 1882
Remarks: E. Brookfield
Pastor: Rev F. A. Bisbee

~ ~ ~ ~ ~ ~ ~ ~ ~ ~ ~ ~ ~ ~ ~ ~ ~ ~

Page: 154   [Line]: [7]
Name: Mrs. Lackey
Date: Nov. 11, 1882
Remarks: E. Brookfield
Pastor: Rev F. A. Bisbee

~ ~ ~ ~ ~ ~ ~ ~ ~ ~ ~ ~ ~ ~ ~ ~ ~ ~

Page: 154   [Line]: [8]
Name: Sheldon Terrill
Date: Dec. 24, 1882
Pastor: Rev F. A. Bisbee
~ ~ ~ ~ ~ ~ ~ ~ ~ ~ ~ ~ ~ ~ ~ ~ ~ ~

Page: 154   [Line]: [9]
Name: Mrs. C. White
Date: Dec. 29, 1882
Pastor: Rev F. A. Bisbee

~ ~ ~ ~ ~ ~ ~ ~ ~ ~ ~ ~ ~ ~ ~ ~ ~ ~

Page: 154   [Line]: [10]
Name: Geo. Monroe
Date: Dec. 31, 1882
Pastor: Rev F. A. Bisbee

~ ~ ~ ~ ~ ~ ~ ~ ~ ~ ~ ~ ~ ~ ~ ~ ~ ~

Page: 154   [Line]: [11]
Name: Mr. Cole
Date: Jan. 1, 1883
Pastor: Rev F. A. Bisbee

~ ~ ~ ~ ~ ~ ~ ~ ~ ~ ~ ~ ~ ~ ~ ~ ~ ~

Page: 154   [Line]: [12]
Name: Baby of Alton Barr
Pastor: Rev J. M. Bartholomew
Additions from Book 2: [on page headed Oct. 1885-Oct. 1886]

~ ~ ~ ~ ~ ~ ~ ~ ~ ~ ~ ~ ~ ~ ~ ~ ~ ~

Page: 154   [Line]: [13]
Name: Baby of Arthur Bacon
Date: 1886
Pastor: Rev J. M. Bartholomew
Additions from Book 2: [on page headed Oct. 1885-Oct. 1886]

~ ~ ~ ~ ~ ~ ~ ~ ~ ~ ~ ~ ~ ~ ~ ~ ~ ~

Page: 154   [Line]: [14]
Name: Mr. Putnam

Date: June 8
Pastor: Rev J. M. Bartholomew
Additions from Book 2: [on page headed Oct. 1885-Oct. 1886]

~~~~~~~~~~~~~~~~~~

Page: 154   [Line]: [15]
Name: Baby of Dennis Cunningham
Date: July 8
Pastor: Rev J. M. Bartholomew
Additions from Book 2: [on page headed Oct. 1885-Oct. 1886]

~~~~~~~~~~~~~~~~~~

Page: 154   [Line]: [16]
Name: Mrs. Cheevar
Date: July 12
Pastor: Rev J. M. Bartholomew
Additions from Book 2: [on page headed Oct. 1885-Oct. 1886]

~~~~~~~~~~~~~~~~~~

Page: 154   [Line]: [17]
Name: Warren Gleason
Date: Jan. 2, 1889
Age: 50
Remarks: E. Brookfield, Unitarian
Pastor: J. S. Gledhill
Additions from Book 2: [Date is listed as date of death in Book 1, but date of funeral in Book 2]

~~~~~~~~~~~~~~~~~~

Page: 154   [Line]: [18]
Name: Mrs. May Wheelock
Date: Jan. 23, 1889
Age: 21
Remarks: E. Brookfield, Unitarian
Pastor: J. S. Gledhill
Additions from Book 2: [Date is listed as date of death in Book 1, but date of funeral in Book 2]

~~~~~~~~~~~~~~~~~~

Page: 154   [Line]: [19]
Name: Chas. Bordwell
Date: May 15, 1889
Age: 56
Pastor: J. S. Gledhill
Additions from Book 2: [Date is listed as date of death in Book 1, but date of funeral in Book 2]; Mrs. Chas. Bardwell listed as deceased

~~~~~~~~~~~~~~~~~~

Page: 154   [Line]: [20]
Name: C. B. Lyon
Date: June 13, 1889
Age: 81
Remarks: No. Spencer
Pastor: J. S. Gledhill
Additions from Book 2: [Date is listed as date of death in Book 1, but date of funeral in Book 2]

~~~~~~~~~~~~~~~~~~

Page: 154   [Line]: [21]
Name: Mrs. Sophia Bullard

Date: Jul. 27, 1889
Age: 64
Pastor: J. S. Gledhill
Additions from Book 2: [Date is listed as date of death in Book 1, but date of funeral in Book 2]; Spencer

~~~~~~~~~~~~~~~~~~

Page: 154   [Line]: [22]
Name: Baby Mr. Horn
Date: Aug. 7, 1889
Remarks: So. Spencer
Pastor: J. S. Gledhill
Additions from Book 2: [Date is listed as date of death in Book 1, but date of funeral in Book 2]

~~~~~~~~~~~~~~~~~~

Page: 154   [Line]: [23]
Name: Job Squires
Date: Oct. 18, 1889
Age: 86
Pastor: J. S. Gledhill
Additions from Book 2: [Date is listed as date of death in Book 1, but date of funeral in Book 2]; Spencer

~~~~~~~~~~~~~~~~~~

Page: 154   [Line]: [24]
Name: J. H. Hathaway
Date: Dec. 7, 1889
Age: 79
Remarks: Charlton
Pastor: J. S. Gledhill
Additions from Book 2: [Date is listed as date of death in Book 1,

but date of funeral in Book 2]; age listed as 77

~~~~~~~~~~~~~~~~~~

Page: 154   [Line]: [25]
Name: T. G. Trott
Date: Dec. 20, 1889
Age: 70
Pastor: J. S. Gledhill
Additions from Book 2: [Date is listed as date of death in Book 1, but date of funeral in Book 2]; Spencer

~~~~~~~~~~~~~~~~~~

Page: 154   [Line]: [26]
Name: Wm. Adams
Date: Jan. 9, 1890
Age: 78
Pastor: J. S. Gledhill
Additions from Book 2: [Date is listed as date of death in Book 1, but date of funeral in Book 2]; Spencer

~~~~~~~~~~~~~~~~~~

Page: 154   [Line]: [27]
Name: Mrs. Julia Payne
Date: Jan. 11, 1890
Age: 32
Remarks: Charlton City
Pastor: J. S. Gledhill
Additions from Book 2: [Date is listed as date of death in Book 1, but date of funeral in Book 2]

~~~~~~~~~~~~~~~~~~

Page: 156   **[Line]:** [1]
Name: Mrs. Charlotte R. Hobbs
Date: Jan. 27, 1890
Age: 74
Remarks: E. Brookfield
Pastor: J. S. Gledhill
Additions from Book 2: [Date is listed as date of death in Book 1, but date of funeral in Book 2]

~~~~~~~~~~~~~~~~~~

Page: 156   **[Line]:** [2]
Name: Miss. A. B. Sherwin
Date: Feb. 13, 1890
Age: 84
Remarks: So. Spencer
Pastor: J. S. Gledhill
Additions from Book 2: [Date is listed as date of death in Book 1, but date of funeral in Book 2]

~~~~~~~~~~~~~~~~~~

Page: 156   **[Line]:** [3]
Name: John Boyden
Date: Mar. 21, 1890
Age: 72
Pastor: J. S. Gledhill
Additions from Book 2: [Date is listed as date of death in Book 1, but date of funeral in Book 2]; Spencer

~~~~~~~~~~~~~~~~~~

Page: 156   **[Line]:** [4]
Name: Leander Sibley
Date: Apr. 10, 1890
Age: 51
Pastor: J. S. Gledhill
Additions from Book 2: [Date is listed as date of death in Book 1, but date of funeral in Book 2]; Spencer

~~~~~~~~~~~~~~~~~~

Page: 156   **[Line]:** [5]
Name: Alvan Bacon
Date: Apr. 15, 1890
Age: 75
Pastor: J. S. Gledhill
Additions from Book 2: [Date is listed as date of death in Book 1, but date of funeral in Book 2]; Spencer

~~~~~~~~~~~~~~~~~~

Page: 156   **[Line]:** [6]
Name: Wm. Barton
Date: Feb. 15, 1890
Age: 26
Remarks: Augusta, Me.
Pastor: J. S. Gledhill
Additions from Book 2: [Date is listed as date of death in Book 1, but date of funeral in Book 2]

~~~~~~~~~~~~~~~~~~

Page: 156   **[Line]:** [7]
Name: Washington Marble
Date: Apr. 16, 1890
Age: 66
Remarks: So. Spencer
Pastor: J. S. Gledhill
Additions from Book 2: [Date is listed as date of death in Book 1, but date of funeral in Book 2]

~~~~~~~~~~~~~~~~~~

Page: 156   [Line]: [8]
Name: Dora A. Barr
Date: Apr. 22, 1890
Age: 7 mo
Pastor: J. S. Gledhill
Additions from Book 2: [Date is listed as date of death in Book 1, but date of funeral in Book 2]; Spencer

~~~~~~~~~~~~~~~~~~~

Page: 156   [Line]: [9]
Name: Jessie Moulton
Date: May 6, 1890
Age: 70
Remarks: E. Brookfield
Pastor: J. S. Gledhill
Additions from Book 2: [Date is listed as date of death in Book 1, but date of funeral in Book 2]; name spelled Jesse Moulton

~~~~~~~~~~~~~~~~~~~

Page: 156   [Line]: [10]
Name: Mrs. Emma Worthington
Date: May 7, 1890
Age: 45
Pastor: J. S. Gledhill
Additions from Book 2: [Date is listed as date of death in Book 1, but date of funeral in Book 2]; Spencer

~~~~~~~~~~~~~~~~~~~

Page: 156   [Line]: [11]
Name: Mrs. Melissa Pike
Date: May 29, 1890
Age: 44
Pastor: J. S. Gledhill

Additions from Book 2: [Date is listed as date of death in Book 1, but date of funeral in Book 2]; Spencer

~~~~~~~~~~~~~~~~~~~

Page: 156   [Line]: [12]
Name: Arthur Barr
Date: June 14, 1890
Age: 45
Pastor: J. S. Gledhill
Additions from Book 2: [Date is listed as date of death in Book 1, but date of funeral in Book 2]; Spencer

~~~~~~~~~~~~~~~~~~~

Page: 156   [Line]: [13]
Name: Mrs. Sallie Clark
Date: June 18, 1890
Age: 76
Pastor: J. S. Gledhill
Additions from Book 2: [Date is listed as date of death in Book 1, but date of funeral in Book 2]; Spencer

~~~~~~~~~~~~~~~~~~~

Page: 156   [Line]: [14]
Name: Charles Dodge
Date: July 11, 1890
Age: 36
Remarks: Charlton
Pastor: J. S. Gledhill
Additions from Book 2: [Date is listed as date of death in Book 1, but date of funeral in Book 2]

~~~~~~~~~~~~~~~~~~~

Page: 156   [Line]: [15]
Name: John D. Brewer
Date: July 28, 1890
Age: 67
Pastor: J. S. Gledhill
Additions from Book 2: [Date is listed as date of death in Book 1, but date of funeral in Book 2]; Spencer

~~~~~~~~~~~~~~~~~~

Page: 156   [Line]: [16]
Name: Baby of M. Howe of Mich.
Date: Oct. 26, 1890
Pastor: J. S. Gledhill
Additions from Book 2: [Date is listed as date of death in Book 1, but date of funeral in Book 2]; infant son of Moses Howe of Mich.

~~~~~~~~~~~~~~~~~~

Page: 156   [Line]: [17]
Name: John Walker
Date: Oct. 30, 1890
Pastor: J. S. Gledhill
Additions from Book 2: [Date is listed as date of death in Book 1, but date of funeral in Book 2]; Spencer

~~~~~~~~~~~~~~~~~~

Page: 156   [Line]: [18]
Name: Miram J. Clark
Date: Nov. 8, 1890
Pastor: J. S. Gledhill

Additions from Book 2: [Date is listed as date of death in Book 1, but date of funeral in Book 2]; name listed as Hiram J. Clarke; Spencer

~~~~~~~~~~~~~~~~~~

Page: 156   [Line]: [19]
Name: Joshua Hill
Date: Jan. 15, 1891
Age: 93
Remarks: Hillsville
Pastor: J. S. Gledhill
Additions from Book 2: [Date is listed as date of death in Book 1, but date of funeral in Book 2]

~~~~~~~~~~~~~~~~~~

Page: 156   [Line]: [20]
Name: Leonard Knight
Date: Apr. 9, 1891
Age: 71
Remarks: Rochdale
Pastor: J. S. Gledhill
Additions from Book 2: [Date is listed as date of death in Book 1, but date of funeral in Book 2]

~~~~~~~~~~~~~~~~~~

Page: 156   [Line]: [21]
Name: Mrs. Lottie Barton
Date: Apr. 17, 1891
Age: 45
Pastor: J. S. Gledhill
Additions from Book 2: [Date is listed as date of death in Book 1, but date of funeral in Book 2]; Spencer

Page: 156   [Line]: [22]
Name: Mrs. Mary A. Sykes
Date: Apr. 26, 1891
Age: 55
Remarks: Wire Village
Pastor: J. S. Gledhill
Additions from Book 2: [Date is listed as date of death in Book 1, but date of funeral in Book 2]

~~~~~~~~~~~~~~~~~~

Page: 156   [Line]: [23]
Name: Charles Bacon
Date: Apr. 29, 1891
Age: 92
Pastor: J. S Gledhill
Additions from Book 2: [Date is listed as date of death in Book 1, but date of funeral in Book 2]; Spencer

~~~~~~~~~~~~~~~~~~

Page: 156   [Line]: [24]
Name: Mrs. Apphia Kelley
Date: June 11, 1891
Age: 39
Pastor: J. S Gledhill
Additions from Book 2: [Date is listed as date of death in Book 1, but date of funeral in Book 2]; Spencer

~~~~~~~~~~~~~~~~~~

Page: 156   [Line]: [25]
Name: Mrs. Mary Hohnberg
Date: July 21, 1891
Age: 56
Pastor: J. S Gledhill

Additions from Book 2: [Date is listed as date of death in Book 1, but date of funeral in Book 2]; Spencer

~~~~~~~~~~~~~~~~~~

Page: 156   [Line]: [26]
Name: Baby of Mr. Henry Copp
Date: Sept. 9, 1891
Pastor: J. S Gledhill
Additions from Book 2: [Date is listed as date of death in Book 1, but date of funeral in Book 2]

~~~~~~~~~~~~~~~~~~

Page: 156   [Line]: [27]
Name: Wm. Barker
Date: Sept. 18, 1891
Age: 67
Remarks: E. Brookfield
Pastor: J. S Gledhill
Additions from Book 2: [Date is listed as date of death in Book 1, but date of funeral in Book 2]

~~~~~~~~~~~~~~~~~~

Page: 157   [Line]: [1]
Name: Etta M. Barr
Date: Oct. 15, 1891
Age: 1
Pastor: J. S. Gledhill
Additions from Book 2: [Date is listed as date of death in Book 1, but date of funeral in Book 2]; Spencer

~~~~~~~~~~~~~~~~~~

Page: 157   [Line]: [2]
Name: Milton H. Howland
Date: Oct. 28, 1891
Age: 14 ½
Pastor: J. S. Gledhill
Additions from Book 2: [Date is listed as date of death in Book 1, but date of funeral in Book 2]; Spencer

~~~~~~~~~~~~~~~~~~

Page: 157   [Line]: [3]
Name: Mrs. S. Luther
Date: Nov. 21, 1891
Age: 76
Pastor: J. S. Gledhill
Additions from Book 2: [Date is listed as date of death in Book 1, but date of funeral in Book 2]; Spencer

~~~~~~~~~~~~~~~~~~

Page: 157   [Line]: [4]
Name: Miss Mary Ryan
Date: Dec. 9, 1891
Age: 33
Remarks: Charlton
Pastor: J. S. Gledhill
Additions from Book 2: [Date is listed as date of death in Book 1, but date of funeral in Book 2]

~~~~~~~~~~~~~~~~~~

Page: 157   [Line]: [5]
Name: Miss Alice I. Prouty
Date: Dec. 15, 1891
Age: 25
Pastor: J. S. Gledhill

Additions from Book 2: [Date is listed as date of death in Book 1, but date of funeral in Book 2]; Spencer

~~~~~~~~~~~~~~~~~~

Page: 157   [Line]: [6]
Name: Miss L. Hill
Date: Dec. 28, 1891
Age: 65
Pastor: J. S. Gledhill
Additions from Book 2: [Date is listed as date of death in Book 1, but date of funeral in Book 2]; alms house

~~~~~~~~~~~~~~~~~~

Page: 157   [Line]: [7]
Name: C. A. Amidon
Date: Jan. 23, 1892
Age: 29
Pastor: J. S. Gledhill
Additions from Book 2: [Date is listed as date of death in Book 1, but date of funeral in Book 2]; Spencer

~~~~~~~~~~~~~~~~~~

Page: 157   [Line]: [8]
Name: Baby of Mr. & Mrs. Hemphill
Date: Feb. 5, 1892
Pastor: J. S. Gledhill
Additions from Book 2: [Date is listed as date of death in Book 1, but date of funeral in Book 2]; Spencer

~~~~~~~~~~~~~~~~~~

Page: 157   [Line]: [9]
Name: Mrs. Deborah H. Adams
Date: Feb. 16, 1892
Age: 63
Remarks: E. Brookfield
Pastor: J. S. Gledhill
Additions from Book 2: [Date is listed as date of death in Book 1, but date of funeral in Book 2]

~~~~~~~~~~~~~~~~~

Page: 157   [Line]: [10]
Name: Andrew Hoe
Date: Apr. 22, 1892
Age: 44
Pastor: J. S. Gledhill
Additions from Book 2: [Date is listed as date of death in Book 1, but date of funeral in Book 2]; Spencer

~~~~~~~~~~~~~~~~~

Page: 157   [Line]: [11]
Name: Mrs. Sarah Wilson
Date: May 28 ,1892
Age: 73
Pastor: J. S. Gledhill
Additions from Book 2: [Date is listed as date of death in Book 1, but date of funeral in Book 2]; Spencer

~~~~~~~~~~~~~~~~~

Page: 157   [Line]: [12]
Name: Ralph Chas. Capen
Date: Jan. 4, 1893
Age: 3 ½ mo.
Remarks: So. Spencer

Pastor: T. O. Marvin
Additions from Book 2: [Date is listed as date of death in Book 1, but date of funeral in Book 2]; Name is Ralph Charters Capen

~~~~~~~~~~~~~~~~~~

Page: 157   [Line]: [13]
Name: Mrs. Arathusa Adams
Date: Jan. 13, 1893
Age: 72
Remarks: E. Brookfield
Pastor: T. O. Marvin
Additions from Book 2: [Date is listed as date of death in Book 1, but date of funeral in Book]2

~~~~~~~~~~~~~~~~~~

Page: 157   [Line]: [14]
Name: Alfred Browning
Date: Jan. 21, 1893
Age: about 80
Pastor: T. O. Marvin
Additions from Book 2: [Date is listed as date of death in Book 1, but date of funeral in Book 2]; Spencer

~~~~~~~~~~~~~~~~~

Page: 157   [Line]: [15]
Name: Mrs. Elizabeth Cook
Date: June 11, 1893
Age: 64
Remarks: So. Spencer
Pastor: T. O. Marvin
Additions from Book 2: [Date is listed as date of death in Book 1, but date of funeral in Book 2]

Page: 157   [Line]: [16]
Name: Thomas Clark
Date: June 9, 1893
Age: 82
Pastor: T. O. Marvin
Additions from Book 2: [Date is listed as date of death in Book 1, but date of funeral in Book 2]; Spencer

~~~~~~~~~~~~~~~~~~

Page: 157   [Line]: [17]
Name: Mrs. Christania Corliss
Date: July 1, 1893
Pastor: T. O. Marvin
Additions from Book 2: [Date is listed as date of death in Book 1, but date of funeral in Book 2]; date could be July 7; Spencer

~~~~~~~~~~~~~~~~~~

Page: 157   [Line]: [18]
Name: James Howland
Date: Sept. 1893
Age: 78
Remarks: E. Brookfield
Pastor: T. O. Marvin
Additions from Book 2: [Date is listed as date of death in Book 1, but date of funeral in Book 2]; age given is 79

~~~~~~~~~~~~~~~~~~

Page: 157   [Line]: [19]
Name: Mrs. Lewis D. Bemis
Date: Oct. 5, 1893
Age: 35
Pastor: T. O. Marvin

Additions from Book 2: [Date is listed as date of death in Book 1, but date of funeral in Book 2]; Spencer

~~~~~~~~~~~~~~~~~~

Page: 157   [Line]: [20]
Name: Chandler Drury
Date: Oct. 15, 1893
Remarks: Husband of Mrs. Adeline Drury, p. 150
Pastor: T. O. Marvin
Additions from Book 2: [Date is listed as date of death in Book 1, but date of funeral in Book 2]; So. Spencer

~~~~~~~~~~~~~~~~~~

Page: 157   [Line]: [21]
Name: Nathaniel Myrick
Date: Dec. 22, 1893
Age: 71
Pastor: T. O. Marvin
Additions from Book 2: [Date is listed as date of death in Book 1, but date of funeral in Book 2]; Spencer

~~~~~~~~~~~~~~~~~~

Page: 157   [Line]: [22]
Name: Mrs. Nancy Sibley
Date: Dec. 24, 1893
Age: 80
Remarks: So. Spencer
Pastor: T. O. Marvin
Additions from Book 2: [Date is listed as date of death in Book 1, but date of funeral in Book 2]

Page: 157   [Line]: [23]
Name: Mrs. Emma Brooks Wilson
Date: Dec. 27, 1893
Remarks: Albany, N. Y.
Pastor: T. O. Marvin
Additions from Book 2: [Date is listed as date of death in Book 1, but date of funeral in Book 2]

~~~~~~~~~~~~~~~~~~

Page: 157   [Line]: [24]
Name: Jason Wilson
Date: Jan. 18, 1894
Age: 69, 11 mo.
Remarks: So. Spencer
Pastor: T. O. Marvin
Additions from Book 2: [Date is listed as date of death in Book 1, but date of funeral in Book 2]

~~~~~~~~~~~~~~~~~~

Page: 157   [Line]: [25]
Name: Mrs. Alice Hastings
Date: Apr. 24, 1894
Age: 75
Pastor: T. O. Marvin
Additions from Book 2: [Date is listed as date of death in Book 1, but date of funeral in Book 2]; Spencer

~~~~~~~~~~~~~~~~~~

Page: 157   [Line]: [26]
Name: S. S. Wiggins
Date: June 28, 1894
Pastor: T. O. Marvin
Additions from Book 2: [Date is listed as date of death in Book 1, but date of funeral in Book 2]; name listed as S. S. Wiggin

~~~~~~~~~~~~~~~~~~

Page: 157   [Line]: [27]
Name: Geo. W. Gibbs
Date: Sept. 19, 1894
Age: 67
Remarks: So. Spencer
Pastor: T. O. Marvin
Additions from Book 2: [Date is listed as date of death in Book 1, but date of funeral in Book 2]

~~~~~~~~~~~~~~~~~~

Name: Mrs. [blank] Hooper
Date: April 3, 1895
Age: 94
Remarks: Cambridge
Pastor: C. W. Biddle
Additions from Book 2: [Found only in Book 2]

~~~~~~~~~~~~~~~~~~

Name: Harry Ellis
Date: April 4, 1895
Age: 35
Remarks: Cambridge
Pastor: C. W. Biddle
Additions from Book 2: [Found only in Book 2]

~~~~~~~~~~~~~~~~~~

Page: 158   [Line]: [1]
Name: Joseph Desoe
Date: Apr. 11, 1895
Age: 74
Pastor: C. W. Biddle

Additions from Book 2: [Date is listed as date of death in Book 1, but date of funeral in Book 2]: Spencer

~~~~~~~~~~~~~~~~~

Page: 158   [Line]: [2]
Name: Mrs. [blank] Bemis
Date: Apr. 26, 1895
Age: 44
Pastor: C. W. Biddle
Additions from Book 2: [Date is listed as date of death in Book 1, but date of funeral in Book 2]; Spencer

~~~~~~~~~~~~~~~~~

Name: Rev. [Clark] R. Moor
Age: 70
Date of Burial: May 1, 1895
Remarks: Cambridge
Pastor: C. W. Biddle
Additions from Book 2: [Found only in Book 2]

~~~~~~~~~~~~~~~~~

Name: Mrs. Nellie N. Wentworth
Date of Burial: May 3, 1895
Remarks: Lynn
Additions from Book 2: [Found only in Book 2]

~~~~~~~~~~~~~~~~~

Name: Alpheus B. Alger
Age: 48
Date of Burial: May 7, 1895
Remarks: Cambridge
Additions from Book 2: [Found only in Book 2]

Page: 1/158   [Line]: [3]
Name: Adaline L. Prouty
Date: May 19, 1895
Age: 75
Pastor: C. W. Biddle
Additions from Book 2: [Date is listed as date of death in Book 1, but date of funeral in Book 2]

~~~~~~~~~~~~~~~~~

Name: David Ellis
Age: 78
Date of Burial: June 18, 1895
Remarks: Cambridge
Additions from Book 2: [Found only in Book 2]

~~~~~~~~~~~~~~~~~

Name: Mrs. Jas. M. Monroe
Age: 80
Date of Burial: June 22, 1895
Remarks: Lynn
Additions from Book 2: [Found only in Book 2]

~~~~~~~~~~~~~~~~~

Name: Jos. R. Pettingill
Age: 80
Date of Burial: July 9, 1895
Remarks: Cambridge
Additions from Book 2: [Found only in Book 2]

~~~~~~~~~~~~~~~~~

Name: Mrs. Mary E. Daniels
Age: 60
Date of Burial: July 27, 1895
Remarks: Cambridge

Additions from Book 2: [Found only in Book 2]

~~~~~~~~~~~~~~~~~

Name: Curtis Merritt
Age: 45
Date of Burial: Sept. 21, 1895
Remarks: Swampscott
Additions from Book 2: [Found only in Book 2]

~~~~~~~~~~~~~~~~~

Name: Mrs. Patience Merriam
Age: 70
Date of Burial: Oct. 8, 1895
Remarks: Cambridge
Additions from Book 2: [Found only in Book 2]

~~~~~~~~~~~~~~~~~

Page: 158   **[Line]:** [4]
Name: Mrs. Julia Hammott
Date: Oct. 16, 1895
Age: 67
Pastor: C. W. Biddle
Additions from Book 2: [Date is listed as date of death in Book 1, but date of funeral in Book 2]; Spencer

~~~~~~~~~~~~~~~~~

Name: Amos H. Burrill
Age: 56
Date of Burial: Nov 16, 1895
Remarks: Lynn
Additions from Book 2: [Found only in Book 2]

Page: 158   **[Line]:** [5]
Name: Mr. Percy Griffin
Date: Nov. 19, 1895
Age: 27
Pastor: C. W. Biddle
Additions from Book 2: [Date is listed as date of death in Book 1, but date of funeral in Book 2]; Spencer

~~~~~~~~~~~~~~~~~

Page: 158   **[Line]:** [6]
Name: Mrs. Julia Frances Gass
Date: Dec. 4, 1895
Age: 63
Pastor: C. W. Biddle
Additions from Book 2: [Date is listed as date of death in Book 1, but date of funeral in Book 2]; Spencer

~~~~~~~~~~~~~~~~~

Name: Anrew H. Godfrey
Age: 53
Date of Burial: Dec. 9, 1895
Remarks: Lynn
Additions from Book 2: [Found only on Book 2]

~~~~~~~~~~~~~~~~~

Page: 158   **[Line]:** [7]
Name: Mr. Franklin Fales
Date: Dec. 26, 1895
Age: 52
Pastor: C. W. Biddle

~~~~~~~~~~~~~~~~~

Name: Mrs. Lucy N. Twitchell
Age: 79
Date of Burial: Jan. 7, 1896
Remarks: Lynn
Additions from Book 2: [Found only in Book 2]

~~~~~~~~~~~~~~~~~~~

Page: 158   [Line]: [8]
Name: Abner Howland
Date: Feb. 6, 1896
Age: 77
Pastor: C. W. Biddle
Additions from Book 2: [Date is listed as date of death in Book 1, but date of funeral in Book 2]; Spencer

~~~~~~~~~~~~~~~~~~~

Name: Mrs. Frances L. Edgeley
Age: 76
Date of Burial: Feb. 10, 1896
Remarks: Cambridge
Additions from Book 2: [Found only in Book 2]

~~~~~~~~~~~~~~~~~~~

Name: Mrs. Cynthia Adams Stacey
Age: 76
Date of Burial: Mar. 2, 1896
Remarks: Lynn
Additions from Book 2: Found only in Book 2

~~~~~~~~~~~~~~~~~~~

Name: Mrs. John Low
Date of Burial: Mar. 24, 1896

Remarks: Lynn
Additions from Book 2: [Found only in Book 2]

~~~~~~~~~~~~~~~~~~~

Name: Mrs. [blank] Trask
Date of Burial: April 21, 1896
Remarks: Cambridge
Additions from Book 2: [Found only in Book 2]

~~~~~~~~~~~~~~~~~~~

Page: 1/158   [Line]: [9]
Name: Israel Taft
Date: May 5, 1896
Age: 76
Pastor: C. W. Biddle
Additions from Book 2: [Date is listed as date of death in Book 1, but date of funeral in Book 2]; Spencer

~~~~~~~~~~~~~~~~~~~

Page: 158   [Line]: [10]
Name: Addison Hobbs
Date: May 7, 1896
Age: 56
Pastor: C. W. Biddle
Additions from Book 2: [Date is listed as date of death in Book 1, but date of funeral in Book 2]

~~~~~~~~~~~~~~~~~~~

Name: Ephraim H. Hyde
Age: 84
Date of Burial: June 20, 1896
Remarks: Stafford, Ct.
Additions from book 2:[Found only in Book 2]

Name: William A. Kidder
Age: 74
Date of Burial: July 2, 1896
Remarks: Cambridge
Additions from Book 2: [Found only in Book 2]

~~~~~~~~~~~~~~~~~

Name: Rev. Geo. Hill
Age: 70
Date of Burial: June 25, 1896
Remarks: [   ]
Additions from Book 2: [Found only in Book 2]

~~~~~~~~~~~~~~~~~

Page: 158   **[Line]:** [11]
Name: Mrs. Mary A. Blodgett
Date: July 19, 1896
Age: 72
Pastor: C. W. Biddle
Additions from Book 2: [Date is listed as date of death in Book 1, but date of funeral in Book 2];
Age: 72 yrs. 7 mo. 5 days

~~~~~~~~~~~~~~~~~

Page: 158   **[Line]:** [12]
Name: Mrs. A. D. Tower
Date: Aug. 31, 1897
Remarks: In absence of F. M. Bissell
Pastor: C. W. Biddle
Additions from Book 2: [Date is listed as date of death in Book 1, but date of funeral in Book 2];
Spencer

~~~~~~~~~~~~~~~~~

Page: 158   **[Line]:** [13]
Name: Samuel E. Rice
Date: Sept. 4, 1897
Age: 53
Remarks: Brookfield
Pastor: F. M. Bissell
Additions from Book 2: Podunk

~~~~~~~~~~~~~~~~~

Page: 158   **[Line]:** [14]
Name: Edwin H. Myrick
Date: Oct. 6, 1897
Age: 47
Pastor: F. M. Bissell
Additions from Book 2: Spencer

~~~~~~~~~~~~~~~~~

Page: 158   **[Line]:** [15]
Name: Harry R. Black
Date: Oct. 24, 1897
Age: 30
Remarks: Hillsville
Pastor: F. M. Bissell

~~~~~~~~~~~~~~~~~

Page: 158   **[Line]:** [16]
Name: Andrew Allen
Date: Dec. 2, 1897
Age: 62
Remarks: So. Spencer
Pastor: F. M. Bissell

~~~~~~~~~~~~~~~~~

Page: 158   **[Line]:** [17]
Name: John Edward Bacon
Date: Feb. 7, 1898
Age: 60
Pastor: F. M. Bissell

Additions from Book 2: Spencer

~~~~~~~~~~~~~~~~~~

Page: 158   [Line]: [18]
Name: Wm. M. Green
Date: Feb. 17, 1898
Age: 25
Pastor: F. M. Bissell
Additions from Book 2:
Spencer; age 25.6

~~~~~~~~~~~~~~~~~~

Page: 158   [Line]: [19]
Name: Julia E. Mills
Date: June 17, 1898
Age: 50
Pastor: F. M. Bissell
Additions from Book 2:
Spencer; age 50.7

~~~~~~~~~~~~~~~~~~

Page: 158   [Line]: [20]
Name: Francis G. Kittridge
Date: June 21, 1898
Age: 40
Pastor: F. M. Bissell
Additions from Book 2: Spencer

~~~~~~~~~~~~~~~~~~

Page: 158   [Line]: [21]
Name: Mrs. Mary A. Pond
Date: Dec. 30, 1898
Age: 50
Date of Burial: Jan. 1, 1899
Remarks: Church member and fine Xtian woman
Pastor: Edward C. Downey

Page: 158   [Line]: [22]
Name: Alfred Wilson
Date: Jan. 21, 1899
Age: 87
Date of Burial: Jan 23
Remarks: Life Long [ ]. Funeral in Church.
Pastor: Edward C. Downey

~~~~~~~~~~~~~~~~~~

Page: 158   [Line]: [23]
Name: Mrs. Geo. Bemis
Date: Sept. 1, 1899
Age: 52
Date of Burial: Sept. 2
Pastor: Edward C. Downey

~~~~~~~~~~~~~~~~~~

Page: 158   [Line]: [24]
Name: Miss Jennie Tremby
Date: Sept. 13, 1899
Age: 17
Date of Burial: Sept. 15
Remarks: Daughter of Mr. & Mrs. J. Tremby
Pastor: Edward C. Downey

~~~~~~~~~~~~~~~~~~

Page: 158   [Line]: [25]
Name: Mrs. J. Lousa Lamb
Date: Feb. 15, 1900
Age: 70
Date of Burial: Feb. 17, 1900
Pastor: Edward C. Downey

~~~~~~~~~~~~~~~~~~

Page: 158   [Line]: [26]
Name: Mrs. P. Bryant

Age: 77
Date of Burial: Dec. 1899
Remarks: Poor Farm
(Congregationalist)
Pastor: Edward C. Downey

~~~~~~~~~~~~~~~~~~

Page: 158   [Line]: [27]
Name: Mr [blank] Wood
Date: Feb. 5, 1900
Age: 31
Date of Burial: Feb. 7
Remarks: Buried in Oakham
Pastor: Edward C. Downey

~~~~~~~~~~~~~~~~~~

Page: 159   [Line]: [1]
Name: Mr. Geo. Walker
Date: Feb. 7, 1900
Age: 71
Date of Burial: Feb. 9
Remarks: Wife a Baptist
Pastor: E. C. Downey

~~~~~~~~~~~~~~~~~~

Page: 159   [Line]: [2]
Name: Geo. E. Clark
Date: Feb. 12, 1900
Age: 66
Date of Burial: Feb. 17
Remarks: G. A. R.
Pastor: E. C. Downey

~~~~~~~~~~~~~~~~~~

Page: 159   [Line]: [3]
Name: Amos Harrington

Date: Mar. 1900
Age: 79
Date of Burial: Mar. 9
Pastor: E. C. Downey

~~~~~~~~~~~~~~~~~~

Page: 159   [Line]: [4]
Name: [blank] Aldrich
Date: Mar. 15, 1900
Age: 41
Date of Burial: Mar. 19
Remarks: Charlton
Pastor: E. C. Downey

~~~~~~~~~~~~~~~~~~

Page: 159   [Line]: [5]
Name: Mrs. Am. Cummings
Date: Apr. 2, 1900
Age: 71
Date of Burial: Apr. 5
Pastor: E. C. Downey

~~~~~~~~~~~~~~~~~~

Page: 159   [Line]: [6]
Name: Mrs. Hattie Babbitt
Date: Apr. 3, 1900
Age: 41
Date of Burial: Apr. 6
Remarks: Buried in Oaxham
[Oakham]
Pastor: E. C. Downey

~~~~~~~~~~~~~~~~~~

Page: 159   [Line]: [7]
Name: Chas. C. Chase
Date: May 13, 1900, Utah
Age: 62
Date of Burial: May 15

Remarks: Buried in New Jersey
Pastor: E. C. Downey

~~~~~~~~~~~~~~~~~~

Page: 159   [Line]: [8]
Name: John Bemis
Date: Sept. 10, 1900
Age: 45
Date of Burial: Sep. 21
Remarks: Son of George Bemis
Pastor: E. C. Downey

~~~~~~~~~~~~~~~~~~

Page: 159   [Line]: [9]
Name: William E. Slayton
Date: Oct. 27, 1900
Age: 77
Date of Burial: Oct. 29
Remarks: Lived in Stoneham, buried in E. Brookfield
Pastor: E. C. Downey

~~~~~~~~~~~~~~~~~~

Page: 159   [Line]: [10]
Name: Edward Bemis
Date: Nov. 7, 1900
Age: 85
Date of Burial: Nov. 9
Pastor: E. C. Downey

~~~~~~~~~~~~~~~~~~

Page: 159   [Line]: [11]
Name: Mrs. Cynthia Bacon
Date: Sept. 29, 1901
Age: 86
Date of Burial: Oct. 2
Remarks: Rev. F. M. Bissell assisted; Burial in Charlton

Pastor: G. W. Fuller

~~~~~~~~~~~~~~~~~~

Page: 159   [Line]: [12]
Name: Mrs. Elvira Howe
Date: Nov. 12, 1901
Age: 81
Date of Burial: Nov. 14
Remarks: Burial in N. Brookfield
Pastor: G. W. Fuller

~~~~~~~~~~~~~~~~~~

Page: 159   [Line]: [13]
Name: Fred Kent Bacon
Date: Dec. 7, 1901
Age: 29
Date of Burial: Dec. 10
Remarks: Burial in Spencer
Pastor: G. W. Fuller

~~~~~~~~~~~~~~~~~~

Page: 159   [Line]: [14]
Name: Wm. Augustus Barr
Date: Dec. 17, 1901
Age: 65
Date of Burial: Dec. 20
Remarks: Burial in Spencer
Pastor: G. W. Fuller

~~~~~~~~~~~~~~~~~~

Page: 159   [Line]: [15]
Name: Mrs. George Bemis
Date: Feb. 24, 1902
Date of Burial: Feb. 28
Remarks: Burial in Spencer
Pastor: G. W. Fuller

~~~~~~~~~~~~~~~~~~

Page: 159   [Line]: [16]
Name: Mrs. A. H. Lovell
Date: June 27, 1902
Age: 54
Date of Burial: June 30
Remarks: Burial in Pine Grove
Cem., Spencer
Pastor: F. L. Masseck

~~~~~~~~~~~~~~~~~~

Page: 159   [Line]: [17]
Name: Mrs. Isabelle E. Phillips
Date: July 28, 1902
Age: 48
Date of Burial: July 30
Remarks: Burial in Worcester
Pastor: F. L. Masseck

~~~~~~~~~~~~~~~~~~

Page: 159   [Line]: [18]
Name: Edgar Abbott
Date: Aug. 7, 1902
Age: 51
Date of Burial: Aug. 9
Remarks: Burial in Paxton
Pastor: F. L. Masseck

~~~~~~~~~~~~~~~~~~

Page: 159   [Line]: [19]
Name: Luther Hill
Date: Aug. 4, 1902
Age: 77
Date of Burial: Aug. 6
Remarks: Burial in Pine Grove
Cem.,   Spencer
Pastor: F. L. Masseck

~~~~~~~~~~~~~~~~~~

Page: 159   [Line]: [20]
Name: Mrs. Lizzie A. Putnam
Date: Aug. 11, 1902
Age: 51
Date of Burial: Aug. 14
Remarks: Burial in Pine Grove
Cem., Spencer
Pastor: F. L. Masseck

~~~~~~~~~~~~~~~~~~

Page: 159   [Line]: [21]
Name: Jarvis M. Bellows
Date: Oct. 17, 1902
Age: 56
Date of Burial: Oct. 20
Remarks: Burial in Holliston,
Mass.
Pastor: F. L. Masseck

~~~~~~~~~~~~~~~~~~

Page: 159   [Line]: [22]
Name: Mrs. Frank T. Prouty
Date: Nov. 1, 1902
Age: 51
Date of Burial: Nov. 4
Remarks: Burial in Pine Grove
Cem., Spencer
Pastor: F. L. Masseck

~~~~~~~~~~~~~~~~~~

Page: 159   [Line]: [23]
Name: Wm. A. Sloane
Date: Jan. 10, 1903
Age: 62
Date of Burial: Jan. 10
Remarks: Burial in Pine Grove
Cem., Spencer
Pastor: F. L. Masseck

Page: 159   [Line]: [24]
Name: Mrs. Sarah Linley
Age: 79
Date of Burial: Jan. 14
Remarks: Burial in Pine Grove
Cem., Spencer
Pastor: F. L. Masseck

~ ~ ~ ~ ~ ~ ~ ~ ~ ~ ~ ~ ~ ~ ~ ~ ~

Page: 159   [Line]: [25]
Name: Thomas A. Prouty
Date: Feb. 14, 1903
Age: 81
Date of Burial: Feb. 16
Remarks: Burial in Pine Grove
Cem., Spencer
Pastor: F. L. Masseck

~ ~ ~ ~ ~ ~ ~ ~ ~ ~ ~ ~ ~ ~ ~ ~ ~

Page: 159   [Line]: [26]
Name: Hazary P. Wilson
Date: Mar. 17, 1903
Age: 81
Date of Burial: Mar. 19
Remarks: Burial in Pine Grove
Cem., Spencer
Pastor: F. L. Masseck

~ ~ ~ ~ ~ ~ ~ ~ ~ ~ ~ ~ ~ ~ ~ ~ ~

Page: 159   [Line]: [27]
Name: Rosalie Bemis
Date: April 7, 1903
Age: 19 mos.
Date of Burial: April 7
Remarks: Burial in Pine Grove
Cem., Spencer
Pastor: F. L. Masseck

~ ~ ~ ~ ~ ~ ~ ~ ~ ~ ~ ~ ~ ~ ~ ~ ~

Page: 160   [Line]: [1]
Name: Joshua Bemis
Date: May 7, 1903
Age: 81
Date of Burial: May 9, 1903
Remarks: Buried in Pine Grove
Cemetery, Spencer
Pastor: F. L. Masseck

~ ~ ~ ~ ~ ~ ~ ~ ~ ~ ~ ~ ~ ~ ~ ~ ~

Page: 160   [Line]: [2]
Name: Job D. Squires
Date: July 14, 1903
Age: 73
Date of Burial: July 16, 1903
Remarks: Buried in Old
Cemetery, Spencer
Pastor: F. L. Masseck

~ ~ ~ ~ ~ ~ ~ ~ ~ ~ ~ ~ ~ ~ ~ ~ ~

Page: 160   [Line]: [3]
Name: Juliet Allen
Date: Aug. 22 [or 24], 1903
Age: 51
Date of Burial: Aug. 24, 1903
Remarks: Buried in Pine Grove
Cemetery, Spencer
Pastor: F. L. Masseck

~ ~ ~ ~ ~ ~ ~ ~ ~ ~ ~ ~ ~ ~ ~ ~ ~

Page: 160   [Line]: [4]
Name: Harry E. Proctor
Date: Oct. 14, 1903
Age: 12
Date of Burial: Oct. 16, 1903
Remarks: Buried in Pine Grove
Cemetery, Spencer
Pastor: F. L. Masseck

Page: 160   [Line]: [5]
Name: Stephen H. Morse
Date: Dec. 12, 1903
Age: 71
Date of Burial: Dec. 15, 1903
Remarks: Buried in Pine Grove
Cemetery, Spencer
Pastor: F. L. Masseck

~~~~~~~~~~~~~~~~~~

Page: 160   [Line]: [6]
Name: Jonas R. Prouty
Date: Dec. 22, 1903
Age: 74
Date of Burial: Dec. 24, 1903
Remarks: Buried in Pine Grove
Cemetery, Spencer
Pastor: F. L. Masseck

~~~~~~~~~~~~~~~~~~

Page: 160   [Line]: [7]
Name: Dennison F. Corliss
Date: Dec. 30, 1903
Age: 66
Date of Burial: Jan. 2, 1904
Remarks: Buried in Pine Grove
Cemetery, Spencer
Pastor: F. L. Masseck

~~~~~~~~~~~~~~~~~~

Page: 160   [Line]: [8]
Name: Charles A. Hill
Age: 50
Date of Burial: Jan. 19, 1904
Remarks: Buried in Pine Grove
Cemetery, Spencer
Pastor: F. L. Masseck

~~~~~~~~~~~~~~~~~~

Page: 160   [Line]: [9]
Name: Mrs. Lawson Prouty
Age: 67
Date of Burial: Feb. 13, 1904
Remarks: Buried in N.
Brookfield
Pastor: F. L. Masseck

~~~~~~~~~~~~~~~~~~

Page: 160   [Line]: [10]
Name: Mrs. Eliza Hale Fay
Age: 74
Date of Burial: Mch. 14, 1904
Remarks: Buried in Greenfield
Pastor: F. L. Masseck

~~~~~~~~~~~~~~~~~~

Page: 160   [Line]: [11]
Name: Everett Walker Livermore
Age: 21
Date of Burial: Mch. 16, 1904
Remarks: Buried in Pine Grove
Cemetery, Spencer
Pastor: F. L. Masseck

~~~~~~~~~~~~~~~~~~

Page: 160   [Line]: [12]
Name: Mrs. Nellie M. Upham
Age: 59
Date of Burial: April 13, 1904
Remarks: Buried in Southbridge
Pastor: F. L. Masseck

~~~~~~~~~~~~~~~~~~

Page: 160   [Line]: [13]
Name: Edward R. Wheeler, M. D.
Age: 65
Date of Burial: May 3, 1904

Remarks: Buried in Pine Grove Cemetery, Spencer
Pastor: F. L. Masseck (assisted)

~~~~~~~~~~~~~~~~~~~

Page: 160   [Line]: [14]
Name: Hiram H. Brewer
Age: 75
Date of Burial: May 22, 1904
Remarks: Buried in Pine Grove Cemetery, Spencer
Pastor: F. L. Masseck

~~~~~~~~~~~~~~~~~~~

Page: 160   [Line]: [15]
Name: Henry F. Barrows
Age: 77
Date of Burial: May 29, 1904
Remarks: Buried in Mount Hope Cemetery, N. Attleboro
Pastor: F. L. Masseck

~~~~~~~~~~~~~~~~~~~

Page: 160   [Line]: [16]
Name: Oscar W. Wilson
Age: 55
Date of Burial: June 14, 1904
Remarks: Buried in Pine Grove Cemetery, Spencer
Pastor: F. L. Masseck

~~~~~~~~~~~~~~~~~~~

Page: 160   [Line]: [17]
Name: Henry S. Hall
Age: 74
Date of Burial: July 18, 1904
Remarks: Buried in Mil[l]bury
Pastor: F. L. Masseck (assisted)

Page: 160   [Line]: [18]
Name: Ellis Worthington
Age: 6 mos.
Date of Burial: Aug. 1, 1904
Remarks: Buried in Pine Grove Cemetery, Spencer
Pastor: F. L. Masseck

~~~~~~~~~~~~~~~~~~~

Page: 160   [Line]: [19]
Name: William Doane
Age: 89
Date of Burial: Aug 4, 1904
Remarks: Buried in Podunk
Pastor: F. L. Masseck

~~~~~~~~~~~~~~~~~~~

Page: 160   [Line]: [20]
Name: Mrs. A. H. Barr
Age: 40
Date of Burial: Sept. 17, 1904
Remarks: Buried in Pine Grove Cemetery, Spencer
Pastor: F. L. Masseck

~~~~~~~~~~~~~~~~~~~

Page: 160   [Line]: [21]
Name: Mrs. Martha B. Lamb
Age: 84
Date of Burial: Sept. 28, 1904
Remarks: Buried in Pine Grove Cemetery, Spencer
Pastor: F. L. Masseck

~~~~~~~~~~~~~~~~~~~

Page: 160   [Line]: [22]
Name: Mrs. Caroline B. Black

Age: 64
Date of Burial: Oct. 10, 1904
Remarks: Buried in Pine Grove
Cemetery, Spencer
Pastor: F. L. Masseck

~~~~~~~~~~~~~~~~~~

Page: 160   [Line]: [23]
Name: Stewart M. Burhan
Age: 2 mos.
Date of Burial: Nov. 6, 1904
Remarks: Buried in Pine Grove
Cemetery, Spencer
Pastor: F. L. Masseck

~~~~~~~~~~~~~~~~~~

Page: 160   [Line]: [24]
Name: Chandler Taft
Age: 84
Date of Burial: Nov. 25, 1904
Remarks: Buried in Old
Cemetery, Spencer
Pastor: F. L. Masseck (assisted)

~~~~~~~~~~~~~~~~~~

Page: 160   [Line]: [25]
Name: Miss Lizzie Gray
Age: ?
Date of Burial: Nov. 28, 1904
Remarks: Buried in Pine Grove
Cemetery, Manchester, N. H.
Pastor: F. L. Masseck

~~~~~~~~~~~~~~~~~~

Page: 160   [Line]: [26]
Name: Lillian D. Mason
Age: 10 days
Date of Burial: Jan. 15,1905

Remarks: Buried in Pine Grove
Cemetery, Spencer, Mass.
Pastor: F. L. Masseck

~~~~~~~~~~~~~~~~~~

Page: 160   [Line]: [27]
Name: Mrs. Amasa Harrington
Age: 78
Date of Burial: Jan. 28, 1905
Remarks: Buried in Pine Grove
Cemetery, Spencer, Mass.
Pastor: F. L. Masseck

~~~~~~~~~~~~~~~~~~

Page: 161   [Line]: [1]
Name: Willard Converse
Age: 72
Date of Burial: Mar. 8, 1905
Remarks: Buried in Old
Cemetery, Spencer
Pastor: F. L. Masseck

~~~~~~~~~~~~~~~~~~

Page: 161   [Line]: [2]
Name: Walter A. Learnard
Date of Burial: Mar. 15, 1905
Remarks: Buried in Pine Grove,
Spencer
Pastor: F. L. Masseck

~~~~~~~~~~~~~~~~~~

Page: 161   [Line]: [3]
Name: Salem Converse
Age: 70
Date of Burial: Mar. 31, 1905
Remarks: Buried in Old
Cemetery, Spencer
Pastor: F. L. Masseck

~~~~~~~~~~~~~~~~~~

Page: 161   [Line]: [4]
Name: Mrs. Susan H[innes]
Morse (Mrs. Stephen H.)
Age: 77
Date of Burial: Apr. 3, 1905
Remarks: Burial in Pine Grove,
Spencer
Pastor: F. L. Masseck

~~~~~~~~~~~~~~~~~~

Page: 161   [Line]: [5]
Name: Albert O. Clark
Age: 42
Date of Burial: Apr. 10, 1905
Remarks: Buried in Pine Grove,
Spencer
Pastor: F. L. Masseck

~~~~~~~~~~~~~~~~~~

Page: 161   [Line]: [6]
Name: Mrs. Edward Walker
Age: 55
Date of Burial: Apr. 26, 1905
Remarks: Buried in Pine Grove,
Spencer
Pastor: F. L. Masseck

~~~~~~~~~~~~~~~~~~

Page: 161   [Line]: [7]
Name: Charles J. Bryant
Age: 67
Date of Burial: May 2, 1905
Remarks: Buried in Holden
Pastor: F. L. Masseck

~~~~~~~~~~~~~~~~~~

Page: 161   [Line]: [8]
Name: John Whitney Houghton

Date: Mar. 30, 1906
Age: 68-2
Date of Burial: Mar. 31
Remarks: Buried in Bolton,
Mass.
Pastor: Asa M. Bradley

~~~~~~~~~~~~~~~~~~

Page: 161   [Line]: [9]
Name: Wm. H. Wilder
Date: May 15, 1906
Age: 61-2
Date of Burial: May 18
Remarks: Buried in Brookfield
Pastor: Asa M. Bradley

~~~~~~~~~~~~~~~~~~

Page: 161   [Line]: [10]
Name: Ruben Adams
Date: May 18, 1906
Age: 88-8-20
Date of Burial: May 20
Remarks: Funeral at late house
in Podunk
Pastor: Asa M. Bradley

~~~~~~~~~~~~~~~~~~

Page: 161   [Line]: [11]
Name: Albert B. Ware
Date: May 30, 1906
Age: 66-0-6
Date of Burial: June 2
Pastor: Asa M. Bradley
~~~~~~~~~~~~~~~~~~

Page: 161   [Line]: [12]
Name: Minnie H. Ross
Date: Sept. 14, 1906
Age: 34-10-11

Date of Burial: Sept. 16
Remarks: Member of Church
(Minnie Howe)
Pastor: Asa M. Bradley

~~~~~~~~~~~~~~~~~~~

Page: 161   [Line]: [13]
Name: Ina Belle Thompson
Date: Dec. 11, 1906
Age: 40-6
Date of Burial: Dec. 13
Remarks: Died at City Hospital,
Worcester, where she had
undergone surgical operation
Pastor: Asa M. Bradley

~~~~~~~~~~~~~~~~~~~

Page: 161   [Line]: [14]
Name: Charles Edgar Graton
Date: Dec. 18, 1906
Age: 60-3-16
Date of Burial: Dec. 21
Remarks: An old soldier
Pastor: Asa M. Bradley

~~~~~~~~~~~~~~~~~~~

Page: 161   [Line]: [15]
Name: Geo. W. Squires
Date: Jan. 13, 1907
Age: 51-1-1
Date of Burial: Jan. 16
Remarks: For two years in
Insane Asylum
Pastor: Asa M. Bradley

~~~~~~~~~~~~~~~~~~~

Page: 161   [Line]: [16]
Name: Rebecca Morrison Bean

Date: Jan. 17, 1907
Age: 80-10-23
Date of Burial: Jan. 19
Remarks: Spinster; native of
Bethel, Me.
Pastor: Asa M. Bradley

~~~~~~~~~~~~~~~~~~~

Page: 161   [Line]: [17]
Name: Theodore P. Green
Date: Jan. 22, 1907
Date of Burial: Jan. 25
Remarks: Died from operation in
Hospital in Boston. Not seen by
relatives for many years.
Pastor: Asa M. Bradley

~~~~~~~~~~~~~~~~~~~

Page: 161   [Line]: [18]
Name: Eliakhim Phelps Cutter
Date: Feb. 13, 1907
Age: 77-2
Date of Burial: Feb. 15
Remarks: Father of Edward P.
Cutter. R. of P. Service.
Pastor: Asa M. Bradley

~~~~~~~~~~~~~~~~~~~

Page: 161   [Line]: [19]
Name: Sarah E. Green
Date: Apr. 6, 1907
Age: 84
Date of Burial: Apr. 9
Pastor: Asa M. Bradley

~~~~~~~~~~~~~~~~~~~

Page: 161   [Line]: [20]
Name: Mrs. Frank A. Smith

Date: Apr. 10, 1907
Age: 58
Date of Burial: Apr. 12
Remarks: East Brookfield
Pastor: Asa M. Bradley

~~~~~~~~~~~~~~~~~~~

Page: 161   [Line]: [21]
Name: Martha A. Wilson
Date: Apr. 22, 1907
Age: 61
Date of Burial: Apr. 25
Remarks: Member of Church.
Died at sanitarium in Burlington,
Vt.
Pastor: Asa M. Bradley

~~~~~~~~~~~~~~~~~~~

Page: 161   [Line]: [22]
Name: Merle S. Nutting
Date: May 31, 1907
Age: 26-2-13
Date of Burial: June 4
Remarks: Died at Epileptic
Hospital, Monson; Funeral from
Mrs. Chandler Drury's, S. Spencer
Pastor: Asa M. Bradley

~~~~~~~~~~~~~~~~~~~

Page: 161   [Line]: [23]
Name: Ebenezer Howe
Date: June 1, 1907
Age: 70-9
Date of Burial: June 13
Remarks: Funeral from Pine
Grove Chapel
Pastor: Asa M. Bradley

~~~~~~~~~~~~~~~~~~~

Page: 161   [Line]: [24]
Name: Nellie L. Stone Prouty
Date: July 24, 1907
Age: 44-9
Date of Burial: July 27
Remarks: Member of Church;
Died at Memorial Hospital,
Worcester
Pastor: F. A. Bisbee

~~~~~~~~~~~~~~~~~~~

Page: 161   [Line]: [25]
Name: Seth J. Adams
Date: Sept. 2, 1907
Age: 40
Date of Burial: Sept. 5
Remarks: Residence Podunk
District; for years an epileptic.
Pastor: A. M. Bradley

~~~~~~~~~~~~~~~~~~~

Page: 161   [Line]: [26]
Name: Mrs. Mary E. Davis
Date: Sept. 15, [1907]
Age: 64-11-15
Date of Burial: Sept. 18
Remarks: Died at the home of
son Geo. W. Davis. Wife of Geo H.
Davis of Worcester.
Pastor: A. M. Bradley

~~~~~~~~~~~~~~~~~~~

Page: 161   [Line]: [27]
Name: Mrs. Mary L. Ware
Date: Oct. 19, [1907]
Age: 63-3-10
Date of Burial: Oct. 21
Remarks: Wife of the A. B. Ware
above
Pastor: A. M. Bradley

~~~~~~

Appendix

~~~~~~

Spencer Massachusetts
March 29. 1909

My dear Mr. Bradley:-

I have this day sent in my application for membership to the Christian Science Church. Please erase my name from the books of the Universalist Church of Spencer and oblige

Yours sincerely,

Ida M Prouty

MISS JENNIE H. SUMNER
MARSHFIELD HILLS
MASSACHUSETTS

1939

To the Universalist Church in Spencer, Mass,
August 8th

Gentlemen :-

Have you any record of the christening of Jennie Henrietta Sumner, soon after the Universalist Church was started in Spencer? My father Lemuel Francis Sumner a druggist was a deacon in the Church, I think Mr. Vail was minister at the time. I remember as a very young child of one of the babies dying and his calling at the house and christening her and mother and father at the time. Suggested that

all of us should be christened,
and as I remember two of us, the
oldest had already been christened
before and of his saying, they
might as well be christened
again.   I was born in
Gloucester, Mass, on June
2nd 1868, Father was Lemuel
Francis Sumner and Mother
Henrietta Gilbert (Plummer) Sumner
but there is no record in the
city records of Gloucester and
as I am applying for Old age
assistance the State insists
there should be more record
than a couple of pages torn from
a little on which my mother kept
the birth records,   awaiting your reply
    I am respectfully   Jennie H Sumner

1939

MISS JENNIE H. SUMNER
MARSHFIELD HILLS
MASSACHUSETTS

August 8th

To the Universalist Church
in Spencer, Mass
Gentlemen:
Have you any record of the christening of Jennie Henrietta Sumner, soon after the Universalist Church was started in Spencer, My father Lemuel Francis Sumner a druggist was a deacon in the church, I think Mr.Vail was minister at the time I remember as a very young child of one of the babies dying and his calling at the house and christening her and mother and father at the time Suggested that all of us should be christened, and as I remember two of us. The oldest had already been christened before and of his saying they might as well be christened again. I was born in Gloucester Mass, on June 2nd 1868. Father was Lemuel Francis Sumner and mother Henrietta Gilbert (Plummer) Sumner, but there is no record in the city records of Gloucester and as I am applying for old age assistance the state insists there should be more record than a couple of pages torn from a bible on which my mother kept the birth records. Awaiting your reply
    I am respectfully   Jennie H. Sumner

~~~~~~

APPENDIX iii
Church Committees

~~~~~~

Loose paper in Book 1, undated:

Sickness:
>Linus H. Bacon
>Phebe C. Johnson
>Mrs. Eleanor J. Davis

Benevolences:
>E. Harris Howland
>Lucy O. Newton
>Mrs. Lois B. Copp

Hospitality & Visitation:
>Deacon Alvan N. Lamb
>Mrs. Edith F. Bacon
>Mrs. Villeroy A. Newton

APPENDIX iv
Y. P. C. U. Members for 1906-07

Linus Bacon
Florence Copp
Fannie Corbin
Eleanor Davis
Alice Hoe
Phebe Johnson
Mary Warren
Mabel White
Frank Barr
Harriet Barr
Ephraim Barr
Julius Sibley
Foster Wheeler
Alvan Lamb
Ruth Macfarland
Mr. Bradley
Mrs. Bradley
Fannie Proctor
[written vertically]
Mrs. Morse
Mrs. Cora Leonard

APPENDIX v
People Who Left Town Without Being Dismissed from the Church

Florence Copp
------ Downey
Carrie Pond
Ruth Sibley
Phebe Johnson
Lori Trask
Jeraldine Prouty
Josephine Prouty
Mary Corbill
Mrs. Goodnow
Antine Goodnow
Nellie Goodnow
Josephine Goodnow

APPENDIX vi
Chicago's Iroquois Theater Fire

On December 30, 1903, a stage curtain at the Iroquois Theater in Chicago burst into flames, resulting in the deaths of over 600 people, mostly women and children. Among them was Clara B. (Robinson) Mills, a 34-year old housewife living at 623 Sedgwick St. with her husband William A. Mills. Clara was a former member of the Universalist Church of Spencer.

As of this writing, the following sites have more information on this horrific fire:

The Chicago Public Library's site, *Absolutely Fireproof: The Iroquois Theater Fire of 1903*, at https://bit.ly/3iOTxFR

The Great Chicago Theater Disaster by Marshall Everett: Clara is missing from the list of the dead
https://archive.org/details/greatchicagothea00everiala/page/n3/mode/2up

The Iroquois Theater Disaster Killed Hundreds and Changed Fire Safety Forever
https://www.smithsonianmag.com/history/how-theater-blaze-killed-hundreds-forever-changed-way-we-approach-fire-safety-180969315/

Find A Grave *Victims of the Iroquois Theatre Fire* virtual cemetery
https://www.findagrave.com/virtual-cemetery/387875

Iroquois Theatre
http://www.iroquoistheater.com/

104

106

111

113